Women, Men and Work: Rural livelihoods in south-eastern Zimbabwe

edited by

Paul Hebinck and Michael Bourdillon

WEAVER
—PRESS—

Published by Weaver Press, Box 1922, Avondale, Harare, 2001.

Typeset by Fontline Electronic Publishing Pvt Ltd, Harare, Zimbabwe.

Cover Design: Jane Shepherd.

Printed by: Modern Press Pvt Ltd, Gweru, Zimbabwe.

The editors and the publisher would like to express their thanks to the Netherlands University Foundation for International Co-operation and the Department of Social Sciences, Wageningen University for their generous support of this publication.

ISBN: 0-77922-003-0

Contents

Preface

This book arises out of co-operation between the University of Zimbabwe and the University of Wageningen in the Netherlands, generously funded by NUFFIC (Netherlands University Foundation for International Co-operation). The project, ZIMWESI (Zimbabwe Programme on Women's Studies, Extension, Sociology and Irrigation), brought together academics from sociology, soil science, irrigation, agricultural economics, and agricultural extension. The aim was to emphasise the importance of combining social factors with technology in development processes, and to improve inter-disciplinary contacts in both teaching and research in these areas.

Most of the chapters in this book arise from research undertaken within the ZIMWESI project. In development studies and planning, people use the term livelihood to emphasise that if we are to understand social processes we need to integrate all aspects of people's lives. The first chapter discusses this concept and its implications. The remaining chapters present case studies that show the importance of such an integrated approach if we are to understand what is happening in rural Zimbabwe.

The material presented here covers a range of topics, including division of labour within families, the use of forest resources, highly capitalised irrigated agriculture, and food processing. All the studies show the importance of examining social issues together with technical ones. The book provides insights for all who are concerned with rural development in general, and in Zimbabwe in particular.

Michael Bourdillon

Chapter 1

Analysis of Livelihood

Paul Hebinck and Michael Bourdillon

Department of Social Sciences, University of Wageningen,
Department of Sociology, University of Zimbabwe

This book is about rural people in Zimbabwe. It is about women, traders, food producers, children and labour migrants and what they do to eke out a living. In their attempts to make a living of some sort, people use a variety of resources such as social networks, labour, land, capital, knowledge and markets to produce food and marketable commodities and to raise their incomes. Their behaviour is not simply determined by culture and social structures: people are agents or actors who are constantly manoeuvring to improve their lives. In these endeavours they become embroiled with others over a range of issues, such as the use of natural resources, rights to land and property, prices for their commodities and even how to understand the world around them. Sometimes negotiations involve institutions and groups, such as extension agencies, family and kinship groups, political parties, tribal authorities and churches. All of these come under the notion of actors. When we talk about livelihoods, we are talking both about resources and the ways in which people manage them in co-operation and competition with others.

The concept of livelihood

'Livelihood' has been coined as an umbrella concept for research as well as for development planning. It involves a framework of analysis that has two main objectives. First, it links holistically the variety of ways by which rural people manage to make a living for themselves within the contexts in which they operate. Second, it attends to the processes that shape these endeavours, and to the activities of institutions and individuals that are external to the communities under consideration, but intervene in the way people try to make a living.

The idea behind this framework can be summarized in the definition formulated by Robert Chambers and Gordon Conway in the mid 1980s, which stated that livelihood

> comprises the capabilities, assets (including both material and social resources) and activities required for a means of living. A livelihood is sustainable when it can cope with and recover from stresses and shock and maintain or enhance its capabilities and assets both now and in the future, while not undermining the natural resource base.[1]

Such a definition links livelihood with people's resources, capabilities and activities, that is, what they do with such resources or assets. We shall return to a discussion of resources later.

The livelihood framework serves a variety of purposes and interests. There has been much criticism of approaches by policy makers that provide a blueprint or preconceived plan for improving the conditions of living for poor countries and poor people. For policy makers, and particularly for the international donor community, 'livelihood' provides a framework that focuses on poverty within the contexts of the people who are poor, and on the processes that underlie poverty. For consultants who operate in the field of development, 'livelihood' represents a framework for the formulation of development projects that focus on the people being affected by the project and the variety of ways in which they might be affected. For social scientists, such as anthropologists, sociologists and economists, 'livelihood' provides a framework for a holistic interpretation of the dynamics of development and the different rhythms of change. For plant breeders, soil scientists and other technologists, the livelihood framework serves the purpose of linking their specific work and capacities with what people are capable of doing, what they are looking for and how they perceive their needs. The livelihood framework thus provides a guide for research and intervention.

'Livelihood' focuses on the fact that the people directly affected by poverty, and by attempts to alleviate it, are striving to make a living, preferably above the level of mere survival. In doing so, they try to create and embrace new opportunities, such as trade and crafts (chapters 4 and 5), food processing (chapters 7 and 8) or even prostitution (chapter 6). At the same time they may have to cope with risks

---

[1]   Quoted in D. Carney (ed.), 'Sustainable rural livelihoods: What contributions can we make?', DFID, London, 1998, p. 4.

and uncertainties, such as erratic rainfall, diminishing resources, pressure on the land, changing life cycles and kinship networks, epidemics such as HIV/AIDS and other diseases, chaotic markets, increasing food prices, inflation, and national and international competition. These uncertainties together with new emerging opportunities impinge on how material and social resources are managed and used, and on the choices people make between different sets of values and identities that are associated with such usage.

Context

Context is fundamental to understanding livelihoods, and is seen as important in all chapters in this book. Context refers not only to broad political and economic structures, but also to the immediate local physical and social environments. Contexts vary enormously, as do development processes. These processes are locally specific, shaped by history, cultural repertoires, economic and political relationships and the natural environment. Livelihood is essentially contextual: livelihoods can only be captured in particular contexts.

For those with few resources, these contexts are often risky, making people potentially vulnerable to shocks, stresses and changes. Changes in growing populations, family composition, governance, technology, health and diseases, as well as changes due to conflict, seasonal variation, drought and pests, impact on what people do and may enlarge or limit their room for manoeuvre. Mate in chapter 3 illustrates how women and children have been adversely affected by changes in economic and family structures. Fragile livelihoods are vulnerable to such shocks and stresses, and poverty makes it hard to influence these conditions. Specific intervention programmes attempt to reduce some aspects of vulnerability: Machiridza and Manzungu show in chapter 8 that these do not necessarily succeed.

During the late 1980s and early 1990s, the livelihood framework specified in more detail the transforming processes and structures that change and shape the contexts in which people try to make a living. The transforming processes and structures thus, directly or indirectly, impinge on people's livelihoods.[2] They operate at various levels. The social level includes changing relationships and the structures of kinship, gender and age. There is a cultural level incorporating customs, religion

---

[2]   D. Carney, 'Sustainable rural livelihoods: What contributions can we make?', DFID, London, 1998; F. Ellis, *Rural Livelihoods and Diversity in Developing Countries*, Oxford University Press, 2000; I. Scoones, 'Sustainable rural livelihoods: A framework for analysis', working paper No. 72, Institute of Development Studies, University of Sussex, 1998.

and other beliefs, including notions of development. The economic level involves investments, global and local markets, prices, international competition and technologies. The political level covers governance and policies, tribal authority, the state, wars and conflicts. It is linked to the judicial level, which covers laws of the state, customary laws and such things as land tenure and rights. The natural environment is also relevant, particularly when natural calamities occur or when the land erodes away. The framework thus aims to link the micro and macro levels of development. It attends to how these interact with each other, and how changes at any level transform what is happening and what is possible at the micro level. This also brings in the necessary dynamic element of change: processes of transformation that shape livelihood contexts.

We should thus be wary of allowing our analysis of livelihoods to be converted into norms for people to follow. The Department for International Development (DFID) for instance argues that,

> the concept of sustainable rural livelihoods is a normative one. DFID aims to improve the lives of poor people and to strengthen the sustainability of their livelihoods... The approach is inherently responsive to people's own interpretations of and priorities for their livelihoods. However... it does not compromise on the environment... What this means is that DFID may not always be in complete harmony with its clients, although, over time, it would hope to become so.[3]

In a similar vein, Ellis claims that the livelihood approach is a framework for policy-making. Both Ellis and DFID refer to some kind of expert knowledge to which the capacity to design policies to reduce poverty can be attributed. In this view, experts seem to have the wisdom and knowledge to judge that a certain livelihood trajectory is more sustainable, or superior, to another. This approach resembles the top-down planning of the latter part of the last century, an approach that perceives markets and technology to be institutions that allocate scarce resources in an optimal way. Farmers who are not using the new technologies, or who prefer to grow their own food crops rather than cash crops in order to protect their means of consumption, are judged to be inefficient. A classic example of such a normative attitude is the assumption that farmers can best develop their farm enterprises by using new technologies, producing crops that are demanded by markets, and particularly by growing crops for which new technologies hold advantages. Attention to the contexts of the farmers, on the other hand, may show that there are good reasons for their choices, and that their actions, where

---

[3]   D. Carney, op. cit., p. 4.

criticized, are sometimes governed by values that override market forces. In this book, we see conflicting perceptions and the failure of imposed norms with respect to natural resources (chapters 4 and 5) and the processing of foods (chapters 7 and 8). We prefer to conceptualize livelihood as a social construct, a way of living built by people who make their own value judgements and who choose to follow a trajectory to fit their own identities.

Resources

Livelihood resources are often categorized as the vital 'capitals' that one needs to achieve a sustainable livelihood.[4] These include:

❖ *human capital* such as labour, skills, knowledge, creativity, experience, drive towards experimentation;

❖ *natural capital* in the form of natural resources like land, water, minerals, crops, forests and pastures;

❖ *physical capital* that can be food stocks, livestock, tools and machinery;

❖ *financial capital* in the form of money, loans or credit; state transfers, remittances, savings; and

❖ *social capital* which concerns the quality of relationships among people and the extent to which one can count on support by the family or mutual assistance.

The coining of social capital serves the idea that livelihoods are seldom constructed on an individual basis only, but rather are embedded in inter-personal networks. There are three core elements that constitute social capital:

❖ *relations of trust, reciprocity and exchange between individuals*, often embedded in specific local forms of organization and shaped by cultural repertoires;

❖ *connectedness, networks and groups*, that include access to wider institutions and so-called 'distant' actors;

❖ *rules, norms and sanctions* that are often, but not always, mutually agreed upon.

---

4   D. Carney, 'Social capital. Key sheets for sustainable livelihoods: Policy, planning and implementation', Department for International Development, ODI, London, 1999; I. Scoones, 'Sustainable rural livelihoods: A framework for analysis', working paper No. 72, Institute of Development Studies, University of Sussex, 1998.

The notion of capital is problematic. One of the problems is that it is an economic metaphor that does not do justice to the nature of people's activities, which are not entirely oriented towards material gain. Although material gains are a very important aim in the notion of livelihood, 'livelihood' does not span only the commoditized world and associated values. The term also incorporates the non-commoditized, non-material, and cultural part of life and sets of values that are embedded in local cultural repertoires. Chapters 4 and 5, for example, look at the ways in which community values determine how and under which conditions forest resources should be used, and how the rights to these resources are embedded in culturally defined relationships. The production of commodities for local and global markets, as opposed to consumption, implies a range of value transformations. In the commodity chain itself, there are shifts in the production of added value as markets change. Commodity production also impacts on social values attributed to other goods, on relationships, on livelihood activities and on forms of knowledge. Commodity production may set off significant cultural transformations in the ways in which social identities are constructed or reconstructed as well as in the ways in which life styles change.[5] Culture is dynamic rather than static, and it is not homogenous.

A further problem is whether to include knowledge in the category of human capital. This would imply that knowledge is an artefact or resource that can be accessed like a commodity. Knowledge is often perceived as being scale and culture neutral, thus universal, and as something that can be developed and applied anywhere. Against this position, knowledge can be perceived as a hybrid phenomenon, neither global nor local. Knowledge becomes localized through a process of redesigning and reworking. It needs to be perceived as a social construct and relationship,[6] rather than as a resource. Bongo in chapter 4 pictures knowledge as an outcome of the social interactions between local strategies that people devise to eke out a living and the political strategies of bureaucratic institutions.

Anyone wishing to contribute to rural people's livelihoods and to reduce poverty must recognize this character of knowledge. The knowledge of outsiders is often met with distrust, frequently confuses local people, and is sometimes not appropriate.

Apart from problems with notions of capital, we need to be wary of simplistic lists of resources. Such resource mapping may be useful but should not be mechanical. Each item on the list must be investigated separately. Whether or not

---

5 N. Long, *An Introduction to the Sociology of Development*, Tavistock Publications, London, 1997.
6 N. Long, *Development Sociology: Actor Perspectives*, Routledge, London, 2001.

a particular resource is present does not tell us about its real or potential usefulness. We need to go beyond the idea that if somebody does not have a certain resource, the resource can be transferred through outside intervention.

Sen introduced the useful concepts of 'endowments' and 'entitlements'.[7] These notions draw attention to two distinct issues: endowments are rights and resources that social actors can have such as land, labour and skills, while entitlements derive from endowments and are what social actors take and receive in practice. The notion of entitlements incorporates issues of power to take command over endowments as well as the capabilities of social actors.[8] The identities of people are derived from what they do with their entitlements. These notions enrich the concept of livelihood with human agency and power as well as with knowledge and social identity.

The discussion on livelihoods can then be enriched with the notion of 'life styles',[9] taking livelihoods beyond the confines of economic activities only. Livelihoods are too often only equated with having a job or with working, and with the various sources of income.[10] The notion of life styles helps us to go beyond such limitations and to incorporate issues pertaining to people's cultural repertoires such as value choices, status, senses of identity *vis-à-vis* other types of actors, and local forms of organization. Mahati and Bourdillon in chapter 7 show how taste and style affect choices of crops and modes of processing. Mate in chapter 3 in particular shows how a variety of values and life styles challenge the idea that human behaviour can be understood with reference only to rationality. Mangoma and Bourdillon in chapter 2 show how values interact with economics in determining the roles of children.

When a life style is based on individuals and groups striving to make a living, livelihoods also include activities both within the locality and stretching beyond it. These activities concern agricultural practices, production of knowledge and gathering information, trading, migratory labour, transport, the search for money via credit schemes or the negotiation of sex. (All of these are illustrated in the chapters of this book.) Wide-ranging interpersonal networks link rural and urban

---

7   A. Sen, *Poverty and Famines. An Essay on Entitlement and Deprivation*, Clarendon Press, Oxford, 1981.
8   M. Leach, R. Mearns and I. Scoones, 'Environmental entitlements: A framework for understanding the institutional dynamics of environmental change', discussion paper No. 359, Institute of Development Studies, University of Sussex, 1996.
9   N. Long, *An Introduction to the Sociology of Development*, Tavistock Publications, London, 1997.
10   F. Ellis, *Rural Livelihoods and Diversity in Developing Countries*, Oxford University Press, 2000; E. Francis, *Making a Living, Changing Livelihoods in Rural Africa*, Routledge, London, 2000; M. Lipton et al., (eds), *Land, Labour and Rural Livelihoods in South Africa*, Indicator Press, Durban, 1996.

areas, on-farm work and off-farm work, and dry-land farming and irrigated farming. Livelihood by definition transcends the boundaries between economic sectors (agriculture as opposed to industry, formal employment as opposed to informal activities). Livelihoods often transcend geographical boundaries, particularly those between urban and rural environments. In other words, people do not live and work only in domains where the boundaries are defined by bureaucracies, like rural and urban, or districts and irrigation schemes, or by natural conditions, such as watersheds or agro-climatic zones.[11] People's livelihoods transcend such domains as they operate in social spaces with boundaries defined by social networks, relationships and identities. These spaces are fluid, constantly changing, and are shaped and constantly re-negotiated by people themselves. They are often understood as arenas since they are subject to struggles and negotiations. More often then not, such arenas also involve the contestation of knowledge – clashes between different bodies of knowledge.

Livelihoods, then, can only be understood by mapping out the various actors (farmers, their families, administrators, traders, extension workers, state institutions and so on), and the networks and social relationships between them. These actors pursue a variety of identities, interests and needs, shaping in turn the particular strategies they devise to improve their conditions of living and their well-being. These strategies are invariably multiple, implying both that there are a variety of ways to sustain a livelihood and that people undertake manifold activities to obtain food, shelter, money and identity. Some of the individual or corporate interests collide and are contradictory. So do their strategies and discourses of development. Development interventions by external agencies, such as state institutions, are often shaped by ideologies of modernization, resulting in a lack of attention to local knowledge, cultural repertoires and practices. Nearly all the chapters in the book bring out this dimension of contestation.

This brings us to understanding rural development. Development in our view is a heterogeneous process involving multiple levels, values and perceived realities, ranging from diverse local patterns of organization and management of natural resources, to regional economic, political and cultural phenomena, intervening state and non-state institutions, development programmes, and global market and political scenarios. At the core lie central issues concerning livelihoods, organizational capacities and discourses, and intervention practices and ideologies. As Long puts it,

---

[11] R. Rhoades, 'Participatory watershed research and management: Where the shadow falls', Gate Keepers Series No. 18, International Institute for Environment and Development, London, 1998.

Rural development represents a complex drama about human needs and desires, organising capabilities, power relations, skills and knowledge, authoritative discourses and institutions, and the clash of different ways of ordering the world.[12]

Development is an arena of struggle in which actors negotiate with each other. Unfortunately, the arena is ordered in such a way that there are winners and losers. The analysis of such processes must not be perceived from a structural or deterministic standpoint.[13] That development processes produce winners and losers does not necessarily mean that the losers remain without any benefit. Although they are structurally positioned as poor, they may well be able to create an unusual livelihood or produce livelihood novelties. These may be hidden in the sense that they are produced by local people but are not noticed by researchers and policy makers. In statistical terms, these hidden novelties represent deviations from the norm. Sometimes they comprise local solutions to particular problems in, for example, soil fertility or crop breeding. If we are to understand the relationship between actors and structures at the micro level, we must pay attention to these hidden novelties .[14]

Livelihood research

Four key issues need attention in livelihood research. These lead into a fifth area of mapping out change.

First, research should start by investigating actor-defined issues. Rather than predetermining the topics to be researched, livelihood research should focus on issues and events that are perceived as relevant and critical by local people, as well as by policy makers, intervening parties, and researchers. This puts researchers in touch with the issues that are real for the people concerned, as well as with specific livelihood domains, action and struggles.

Second, livelihood research must map out the actors that are relevant to such events. This entails identifying the relevant social units and fields of activity. One should not prejudge the issue, as many studies do, by fixing upon the more

12   N. Long, *An Introduction to the Sociology of Development*, Tavistock Publications, London, 1997, p. 2.
13   N. Long and J. D. van der Ploeg, 'Heterogeneity, actor and structure: Towards a reconstitution of the concept structure', in D. Booth (ed.), *Rethinking Social Development: Theory, Research and Practice*, Longman, London, 1994.
14   H. Wiskerke and J. D. van der Ploeg (eds), *The dynamics of agricultural innovation at the interface of novelty creation and socio-technical regimes*, Van Gorcum, Assen, (forthcoming).

conventional anchorage points for an analysis of social and economic life such as the 'household', the 'local community', the 'production sector', the 'commodity chain' and so on. The 'household', for example, often does not reflect a single social unit and the concept conceals a variety of interests and alliances. This is well illustrated in chapter 3 on family and inheritance and in chapter 2 on children. The notion of 'headship' may likewise conceal a variety of decision-making processes.[15] Community' may be a political and ideal construct, and is very often more heterogeneous than is assumed. Most of the studies in this book draw attention to competing interests within communities. 'Production' cannot be disconnected from 'reproduction' and 'consumption'.[16] We should not assume homogeneity in populations, communities or within households themselves. Social categories are differentiated according to class, status, gender, ethnic origin and age. The relevant categories can only be defined and agreed upon through a process of enquiry at community level that incorporates the perceptions and observations of the people themselves, and that acknowledges their different interests and internal conflicts.

Third, we need to document what actors do, their social practices and strategies and the ways in which their actions impact on the use of resources. This includes the mapping of the interpersonal networks in the pursuit of a livelihood. We have to see livelihoods as not simply individual concerns but as built-on relationships with others who may have markedly different lifestyles. These relationships bridge various social spaces that constitute the social basis of livelihoods. Livelihood research thus needs to transcend local communities in order to comprehend both the internal relationships within any unit and significant relationships with other units as they change over time. These relationships stretch geographically over considerable physical distances.

Such relationships and the strategies that they involve are not easily captured in either large or small-scale surveys based on single interviews with the so-called 'head of the household'. Rapid participatory research in any one community may also overlook these linkages. The methodology adopted by all the studies in this book combines participant observation, repeated visits and interviews of different household members, wherever they are. In addition, case studies of individuals bring out the strategies that are devised to create a livelihood.

---

15   J. Guyer, 'Household and community in African studies', *African Studies Review*, Vol. 24, No. 2/3, 1981, pp. 87-138; C. Murray, 'Changing livelihoods in Qwaqwa: Research questions and methods of study', in 'Multiple livelihoods and social change', working paper No. 1, Institute for Development Policy and Management, Manchester University, 1998.
16   J. D. van der Ploeg, *Labor, Markets and Agricultural Production*, Westview Press, Boulder, 1990.

These strategies are expressed or contained in narratives, either written or spoken, which represent people's ideals and constraints. The narratives also reflect the life styles of individuals and groups and the specific ways in which identities are constructed. Folk concepts in narratives inform us how the world is socially ordered. Thus narratives comprise an important part of livelihood research.

A fourth element in livelihood research is identifying and analysing constraints and opportunities, as well as the potential and real shocks for certain livelihoods. It is important to look at how these constraints, opportunities, shocks and stresses affect people's livelihoods; how and why these constraints and opportunities have changed over time, and how actors have responded to such changes. A crucial aspect of this is an analysis of the kind of interfaces and struggles that emerge when different life worlds encounter one another. The analysis necessarily includes not only the local or target groups but also institutional actors and other stakeholders such as donors, governments, extension agents, traders, and village leaders. At this point, one can elucidate the processes of knowledge and power, including how people negotiate and how they rework or redesign certain interventions. One can capture concretely how certain intended consequences go together with unintended consequences. The literature provides good examples of this kind of research.[17]

A further possible step for livelihood research is to begin to map out the possible scenario for change and development. The chapters in this book point to problems created when development agencies fail to pay sufficient attention to the livelihoods of the people they study. This may be due to the fact that such agencies fail to take account of different interests within households, their use of technology or their perceptions of what is necessary or sustainable in their lives.

Most forms of development involve the welding of local opportunities with resources from outside. Development does not merely happen in localities, but also across localities. Each has its own distinctive composition of labour power, skills, knowledge, experiences and endowments. It is, therefore, inevitable that development processes are shaped by local factors.[18] Development becomes

---

[17] K. Crehan and A. van Oppen, 'Understanding of "development": An arena of struggle. The story of a development project in Zambia', *Sociologia Ruralis*, Vol. 28, No. 2/3, 1988, pp. 113-146; J. P. De Sardan, 'Peasant logics and the development project logics', *Sociologia Ruralis*, Vol. 28, No. 2/3, 1988, pp. 216-226; R. Mongbo, 'The appropriation and dismembering of development intervention. Policy, discourse and practice in the field of rural development in Benin', Ph.D. thesis, Wageningen University, 1995.

[18] P. Lowe *et al.*, 'Networks in rural development. Beyond exogenous and endogenous models', in J. D. van der Ploeg and G. van Dijk (eds), *Beyond Modernisation. The Impact of Endogenous Development*, Van Grocum, Assen, 1995, p. 93.

theoretically as well as practically a particular balance of internal and external elements.[19]

There is no blueprint for development and change. The time is past that we, as outsiders, devise plans for development that we expect others to follow. Alternative frameworks have emerged such as 'planning from below' or 'participatory planning'.[20] Common to these perspectives is to incorporate into the planning process the people at whom development is aimed.

Although we have no simple blueprint for development, we can give some general, guiding design principles. First, it is important to view the planning from below as inter-disciplinary, integrating the technical and socio-cultural dimensions of livelihoods.

Second, there are a variety of ways of dealing with any problem, not all of which are reconcilable with each other. People respond differently to change, with different interests and life styles, making consensus unlikely. Development is essentially a non-linear process, contradictory and heterogeneous in nature. Consequently the heterogeneous nature of development is linked with human agency, and development planning needs build on the variety of local practices.

A third principle requires a critical analysis of the available local (endogenous) and external (exogenous) resources, whether used or not, and of how these resources are combined in practices that are relevant to rural people. In particular, we should be looking for the hidden novelties. A critical issue here is what particular exogenous resources are required to strengthen the deployment of endogenous resources, and how these exogenous resources need to be brought in. This analysis would also include a critical review of current agrarian policies.

The authors of the chapters within this book are concerned with development. Although we have no blueprints for development, we do point out problems that arise when development planning pays insufficient attention to the livelihoods of the people who are supposed to benefit. We point out that there are conflicting local interests within communities, conflicting knowledge and perceptions, conflicting strategies and ideals, and conflicting social and economic situations. All these are relevant to understanding how actors try to shape their own livelihoods.

---

[19] J. D van der Ploeg and A. Long (eds), *Born From Within. Practice and Perspectives of Endogenous Rural Development*, Van Gorcum, Assen, 1994, p. 4.
[20] R. Chambers, *Whose Reality Counts? Putting the First Last*, Intermediate Technology Publications, London, 1997.

Chapter 2

The Work of Children in Impoverished Families

Jackie Mangoma and Michael Bourdillon
Department of Sociology, University of Zimbabwe

In this chapter, we examine the role of children within poor households in Biriwiri in Chimanimani District, focusing on the work they do within the family. We show how children contribute to household livelihoods, and constitute a particular interest group within households. This contribution together with the traditional ideology influences the way 'childhood' is constituted as well as the roles allocated to children. This chapter also looks at how children see and respond to their roles, having a limited ability to negotiate them.

A child is primarily part of a domestic group that determines most of his or her activities.[1] Daily insecurity, economic hardship and shortage of labour of rural families have all contributed to boys and girls sharing in household work at an early age. Children of rural families engage in variety of activities that, though seldom enumerated, are necessary for the livelihood of the family.

Although much has been written about child labour where children are involved in paid employment, it is only relatively recently that scholars have focused on child work within the domestic sphere. Nieuwenhuys[2] comments that the study of child work within the household has been neglected because it does not normally impair the healthy development of children nor does it detract from essential activities such as education and play. While waged employment is often seen to involve the objectionable exploitation of children, work undertaken under parental

---

[1]   A. James et al., *Theorising Childhood*, Polity Press, Cambridge, 1998, p. 20.
[2]   O. Nieuwenhuys, *Children's Lifeworlds: Gender, Welfare and Labour in the Developing World*, Routledge, London, 1994, p. 3.

supervision is seen to be part of the household's moral economy and an essential part of socialization. Nieuwenhuys points out that work within the household is not always morally neutral, and deserves more attention than it has received in the past.

We need to notice that the way people view child work within the household depends on their culture, which is the result of particular historical processes. Child work is viewed as an important vehicle for conveying societal knowledge and skills. While such perceptions are, like all ideologies, grounded in reality, they also reflect the interests of those who are in control. The role of children within rural households has come to be shaped by ideologies that serve the interest of the parents and society.

There is another point that we need to take into account when studying children. Jones[3] comments that what at face value appear to be ethnographic accounts of children's lives are usually explorations of adult institutions, adult perceptions and the cultural logic that lies behind them. Adults and adult culture remain the real subjects of study and children are merely the medium of enquiry. Research on children should focus on the views and perceptions of children. We need to recognize that children have their own creative perspectives that contribute to the social fabric in which they live. While parents' views were not ignored, this study gave primacy to children.

Role of children within the agricultural economy

While children are generally important in any household, they have particular importance within families that lack resources. The labour of children is crucial where there are no state welfare payments and where self-employment and low incomes are widespread.[4] This is especially the case where the household head is unemployed. When a parent is sick or disabled, children take on major responsibilities.[5]

Several factors contribute to the allocation of work to children. A general explanation has been that poverty accounts for children's roles in labour force. We

---

3   S. Jones, *Assaulting Childhood: Children's Experiences of Migrancy and Hostel Life in South Africa*, Witwatersrand University Press, Johannesburg, 1993, p. 27.
4   A. James et al., *Theorising Childhood*, Polity Press, Cambridge, 1998, p. 106.
5   J. Aldridge and S. Becker, *Children who care: Inside the world of young carers*, Department of Social Sciences, Loughborough University, 1993, p. 112.

need also to acknowledge other factors, such as traditional social values, shortage of labour and economic hardships. Where children work full time, their labour is seen as a resource that can contribute to the family's survival. This notion of survival is not solely linked to a family's economic poverty. In regions with little or no developed infrastructure, a child's contribution may be to carry out time-consuming tasks that would otherwise remove adults from other necessary tasks.

Country reports from Africa and Latin America show that children are widely involved in agriculture.[6] This is often in subsistence farming where children participate along with the rest of the family in the production of food. In Zimbabwe, 26 per cent of children aged between five and seventeen are involved in economic activities. Most of this is unpaid family work. Only 8.7 per cent work more than three hours a day. Ninety per cent of working children live in rural areas.[7] Some carry out traditional activities at precarious subsistence levels. Other children are involved in commercial, export-oriented plantations of coffee, fruit, flowers and sugar cane. The poor tend to live in areas that are marginal for agriculture because of low production, rough terrain and lack of irrigation. Many indigenous people lost their fertile lands and water rights on the onset of colonialism.

In rural areas, there has traditionally been little differentiation between productive and domestic work. Both have been seen as children's responsibilities, perhaps as their rights. Work is an important vehicle for conveying knowledge about one's community, environment and society. The norms and pace of this kind of education are established culturally to ensure children's development is suited to their environment and maturation.[8] Consequently, at a very young age, children begin to 'help' their parents with both routine household chores and 'productive' activities.

Reynolds[9] points out that in rural areas of Zimbabwe children as young as five help their parents by tending small animals and participating in off-farm activities. As they grow older, these children assume other tasks during planting and harvesting. At the onset of adolescence, they take on work that is differentiated according to gender. Boys perform tasks that require greater physical strength, while girls concentrate on household work.

---

6   J. McKechnie and S. Hobbs, 'Working children: Reconsidering the debates', a report of the International Working Group on Child Labour, Defence for Children International, and the International Society for the Prevention of Child Abuse and Neglect, 1998, p. 20.

7   Government of Zimbabwe, *Zimbabwe 1999 National Child Labour Survey*, Central Statistical Office, Harare, 1999, pp. xii, 53.

8   A. James, *et al.*, op. cit., p. 6.

9   P. Reynolds, *Dance Civet Cat: Child Labour in the Zambezi Valley*, Zed Books, London, 1991.

In the current economic climate of Zimbabwe, poor families are coming under increasing economic strain. There is rapid inflation and widespread unemployment in the country. While basic needs, like clothing, schooling and many foods, require an ever-increasing cash income, the possibilities of acquiring cash are decreasing. In order to cope with this harsh economic climate, parents engage the services of their children in the day-to-day running of the household. This study illustrates Jones' general point[10] that when parents come under particularly intense economic stress, children may be perceived as an immediate available way of alleviating their financial problems. Thus economic factors that stem from international world markets have an impact on the lives of children in the rural areas.

The work that children engage in, even within the home, can damage their health and inhibit social and physical development. This may result from the arduous nature of the work or contact with harmful substances, especially chemicals in agriculture. More frequently, it detracts from creative leisure activities and from the schoolwork of the children.

Although many children, perhaps most of them, work and attend school, there is evidence that work adversely affects school performance, especially for the poorest children.[11] Working children often drop out of school, repeat classes, fall behind or fail and have generally low academic achievement. We shall see that for some of the children in this study, work interferes with schooling but also that it makes schooling possible.

Methodology

Mangoma stayed in Biriwiri in January and part of February 1999 to carry out this investigation. She obtained information from the children themselves, as well as their families, their schools and others in the community. She observed the children at home and at work to get an idea of the extent of their contribution to family livelihood. She also hired assistants to continue observations after she had left the area.

---

[10] S. Jones, *Assaulting Childhood: Children's Experiences of Migrancy and Hostel Life in South Africa*, Witwatersrand University Press, Johannesburg, 1993.
[11] M. C. Salazar and W. A. Glasinovich, (eds), 'Better Schools, Less Child Work: Child Work and Education in Brazil, Columbia, Ecuador and Guatemala', International Child Development Centre, UNICEF, Florence, 1998, p. 111.

After a short observation of ten households that lacked resources, four were selected for further study. The first case was a polygamous unit. The second was centred on orphans staying with guardians who were unemployed, sick, elderly and lacked resources for viable agricultural production. The third comprised children who lived with very poor parents in a monogamous situation. In the fourth case, there were also other marginalized kin who impinged on the lives of the children. A fifth case was selected from better-off families by way of comparison.

All names used in this chapter are pseudonyms.

Biriwiri

The area called Biriwiri is named after the river that flows through it. It is very mountainous, reaching from an altitude of 1,957 metres at the highest point down to 870 metres where the Biriwiri flows into the Nyanyadzi River. Slopes of 50 per cent are no exception. Most of Biriwiri has a climate classified as moderately or well suited to agriculture, with a small part having higher rainfall. Originally most of the catchment area was covered with woodlands and forest.[12]

The main crops are maize, beans, sunflower, sorghum and millet. Much of the area is not arable and is used for grazing and to collect wood for fuel and for construction purposes. Woodlands also provide materials for crafts (see chapter 4 in this volume). A tarred road crosses through the catchment from Wengezi to Chimanimani, the main link between this district and the rest of the country. Biriwiri has a clinic, a mission with a secondary school, four primary schools and electricity and tap water.

Most people living in Biriwiri are Shona, though not all belong to the Ndau people who originally occupied these areas. Many of the families have lived in the area since the 1950s. These are the important families in the area. The largest is the chief's family, the Muusha family.

Most families depend, partly or completely, on agriculture for their survival. Some have people earning wages outside the area. Others operate shops within the area to supplement their income. Shop owners are generally more wealthy. Although rich, not all of them are regarded as important.

---

12   K. A. Bromley, *et al.*, 'Melsetter Regional plan', Department of Conservation and Extension, Harare, 1968.

The people with the largest influence are active within the community or the church. They have stayed in the area for a long time, gained the trust of their fellow villagers and invested time in keeping good relations with them. Within Shona society, authority lies with older people. In most cases family and community leaders ultimately take the most important decisions on the role and welfare of children within the community.

The children

Children in a polygamous household

The Maushe family is a polygamous unit: Mr Maushe has three wives and seventeen children, and his father lives with the family. He used to work on tea and coffee plantations near Chipinge, but now lives on the land. Until recently he belonged to an apostolic church which allowed polygamy. Catherine is twelve years old and in Grade 6 at Biriwiri Primary School. She is the oldest in her mother's household. She is a working child even though she does not frequently enter waged employment.

Catherine has to perform various tasks within the household, including washing clothes, cooking, helping regularly in the field (weeding, planting and harvesting), fetching firewood and water and looking after the younger siblings. She also sweeps the yard and is occasionally involved in waged labour in the form of piecework. Sometimes she collects firewood to sell to the teachers at the mission. She charges $10 for a bundle of about five logs.

During the study, Catherine was observed doing most of the chores. She was observed on two days, a Monday and a Saturday.

Catherine: Monday

Time	Tasks	Total working hours
5.30 a.m. – 6.00 a.m.	Gathering firewood	30 minutes
6.00 a.m. – 6.15 a.m.	Preparing the fire	15 minutes
6.15 a.m. – 6.35 a.m.	Cleaning	20 minutes
6.35 a.m. – 7.00 a.m.	Washing plates	25 minutes
7.30 a.m. – 1.00 p.m.	School	
1.30 p.m. – 2.15 p.m.	Washing plates	45 minutes
2.15 p.m. – 3.00 p.m.	Fetching water	45 minutes
3.00 p.m. – 5.00 p.m.	Weeding in the field	2 hours
5.00 p.m. – 6.00 p.m.	Preparing for evening meal	1 hour
6.00 p.m. – 6.35 p.m.	Bathing the younger siblings	35 minutes
		6 hours 35 minutes

Catherine: Saturday

Time	Tasks	Total Hours
6.00 a.m. – 6.15 a.m.	Preparing the fire	15 minutes
6.15 a.m. – 6.50 a.m.	Cooking porridge	35 minutes
7.00 a.m. – 7.30 a.m.	Washing plates	30 minutes
7.30 a.m. – 8.00 a.m.	Cleaning the house	30 minutes
8.00 a.m. – 8.45 a.m.	Sweeping the yards	45 minutes
8.45 a.m. – 11.45 a.m.	Weeding in the field	3 hours
12.00 p.m. – 12.25 p.m.	Fetching water	25 minutes
12.30 p.m. – 1.45 p.m.	Preparing lunch	1¼ hours
2.05 p.m. – 2.30 p.m.	Cleaning dishes	25 minutes
2.20 p.m. – 5.00 p.m.	Collecting firewood	2½ hours
5.00 p.m. – 6.00 p.m.	Helping in evening meal preparations	1 hour
		11 hours 10 minutes

Working week approximately 46 hours[13]

---

[13]   To calculate the working week, we multiplied the work done on a school day by five, added the Saturday, and assumed minimal domestic work of two hours on Sundays for girls and one hour for boys. The work was sometimes relaxed, and included odd short breaks and slow ambling when chores required walking.

Catherine commented that she faces problems as a working child. During the growing season the heat affects her, resulting in her nose bleeding. She said that she sometimes complains but this does not help. She has to do the work, rest when she is tired and then continue working. Other problems she encounters include lack of school fees, stationary, uniforms and clothing. She sometimes engages in contract labour to help raise money for her school fees. She was placed fifth in her class in Grade 5. She commented that she did not have time to read at home because she has to perform the various chores. 'My work is important in the household because I help my parents with most of the work, making it easier for them,' she said.

We also interviewed Gregory, who is aged fifteen and in Grade 7. He is the son of Mr Maushe's first wife and the third-born in this household. Gregory helps plough the field and weed the crops. He also herds the goats, fetches water and firewood, and washes his own clothes and those of the other family members. Gregory's working hours were also observed for two days, a Tuesday and a Saturday.

Gregory: Tuesday

Time	Tasks	Total Hours
5.30 a.m. – 6.50 a.m.	Fetching water Chopping firewood	1 hour 20 minutes
7.30 a.m. – 1.00 p.m.	School	
2.30 p.m. – 5.45 p.m.	Weeding in the field Fetching water	3 hours 15 minutes
		4 hours 35 minutes

Gregory: Saturday

Time	Tasks	Total Hours
5.00 a.m. – 11.00 a.m.	Weeding in the fields	6 hours
12.00 p.m. – 1.00 p.m.	Fetching water	1 hour
2.00 p.m. – 3.00 p.m.	Working in the garden	1 hour
4.00 p.m. – 6.00 p.m.	Collecting firewood	2 hours
		10 hours

Working week approximately 33½ hours

Gregory said that sometimes he does work like ploughing without having eaten anything. He added that there is no one to help him do most of the chores. Other problems he mentioned were lack of books, school fees, food and clothing and going to school late sometimes because he has to finish his chores first. This is the case with ploughing during the planting season.

Gregory said that the previous year Gregory used to do piecework and could earn up to $10, for a day's work of weeding about a third of an acre. At the time of the study, however, he was unable to do piecework because of the heavy workload within the household. He regularly sells firewood to the schoolteachers at the mission. The money he earns is used to supplement his school fees and buy pencils, pens and notebooks. He said, 'I play an important role within my family because my parents depend on me for doing some of the household chores.'

Children's work is seldom an individual strategy. The chores they undertake benefit not only themselves, but also the whole family.

Tinotenda and Tafadzwa illustrate the young age at which children start work, and the cultural factors that influence their work. Tinotenda and Tafadzwa are twins in the Mausha family. They are six years old and not yet at school. They occupy the fifth-born place in the first wife's household. Tinotenda, a boy, helps fetch water and firewood, herds the goats and chases the baboons from the fields. Some of the interviews with him took place when he was guarding the fields. He commented that he gets tired doing his chores and so he also resorts to playing at work, but sometimes he refuses to do the chores allocated to him. His girl twin, Tafadzwa, helps look after her younger siblings while her parents are doing their work. She also collects small sticks of firewood, and helps wash plates and sweep.

Orphans as part of the household economy

The second case study involves orphans. Tinashe is 13 years old. His parents died when he was seven. He has one brother, aged fifteen. They stay with their father's brother, Mr Sanyika, who is the guardian of the orphans. He is 42 years old and does not work. Mr Sanyika stays with his father, who is very old and sick. Like children who stay with their parents, orphans also have various tasks that they have to perform within their households.

Tinashe's household chores include fetching water, weeding in the field, collecting firewood, doing the laundry and cooking. He also ploughs the fields. He says that there is no one to help him with his daily chores, which corresponds with our observations. He says that his brother, Fanuel, used to help him before he went to work in Rusitu. Tinashe says that he does not complain when doing the chores because even if he does there is no one to help him.

When asked about problems, Tinashe said that he did not have things like soap, clothes, school fees, school uniform and shoes. Tinashe went to school without a uniform. Mr Sanyika, the guardian, said that the orphans lacked clothing and so sometimes he took his own trousers and made them into shorts for the young boys. This was true as observed from Tinashe's clothing.

Tinashe is also involved in waged labour at Pachedu, where he picks coffee and tea. He picks coffee during the school holiday and weekends. Labourers are paid according to the amount they pick. This works out at an average of between $6 and $8 a day. During the growing season, Tinashe also does piecework after school. This earns him between $5 and $10 a day. He uses his income to pay school fees and buy stationary. On the problems encountered while picking coffee, Tinashe says sometimes he goes to work without having any food. He said picking coffee is very painful because pickers have to bend and sometimes they can fall from the ladder they are using, as he once did. He says that plantation owners are fair in their payments because they pay according to the amount of coffee picked and not according to the worker's age. On a good day, Tinashe can earn $20-30. He gives some of his money to his uncle, who uses it for the household.

Tinashe had not yet paid school fees for the current term but in previous years he paid his fees. He said that his uncle sometimes helped him to raise the required amount. Tinashe was observed on two consecutive days, a Friday and a Saturday. On the Saturday morning, he earned $25 for weeding about 30 lines, an area measuring 70 metres by 70 metres.

Tinashe: Friday

Time	Task	Total Hours
5.10 a.m. – 5.50 a.m.	Cleaning the household	40 minutes
5.50 a.m. – 6.20 a.m.	Preparing firewood	30 minutes
6.20 a.m. – 7.05 a.m.	Cooking	45 minutes
7.30 a.m. – 1.00 p.m.	School	
2.20 p.m. – 3.30 p.m.	Fetching firewood	1 hour 10 minutes
3.45 p.m. – 4.30 p.m.	Fetching water	45 minutes
5.00 p.m. – 5.30 p.m.	Washing plates and utensils	30 minutes
6.00 p.m. – 7.20 p.m.	Preparing evening meat	1 hour 20 minutes
		5 hours 40 minutes

Tinashe: Saturday

Time	Task	Total Hours
5.30 a.m. – 8.30 a.m.	Cleaning the household	40 minutes
	Preparing firewood	30 minutes
	Fetching water	50 minutes
	Cooking	40 minutes
9.00 a.m. – 12.30 p.m.	*Maricho* – weeding at one of the local plots	3 hours 30 minutes
2.00 p.m. – 5.30 p.m.	*Maricho*	3 hours 30 minutes
		9 hours 40 minutes

Working week approximately 39 hours

Tinashe says that his life has changed since his parents died. He says that when his father was alive, he used to do less work and they had most of the resources they needed like food and clothing. Tinashe values his work within the household because if he were not there his uncle and grandfather would have problems. He says he has no hopes or aspirations for the future and will drop out of school as soon as he finishes his Grade 7 because there is no one to pay for his secondary education.

On health, Tinashe says that he mostly gets affected by influenza and coughing and he has to walk for treatment to the clinic, which is about seven kilometres away. He says,

My life is different from most children in Biriwiri because these children have a mother and a father, so it makes all the difference in the world. I also have a big responsibility because my uncle and grandfather are always sick and so I have to help them by cooking for them, fetching water for them to bath, washing their clothes, ploughing, planting and harvesting our small plot. All these things I have to do. I cannot refuse.

We visited Tinashe when he was weeding on their small plot of less than an acre. Tinashe says that the harvest is usually low and so the uncle's older children sometimes bring groceries and clothing. Tinashe also gets helps from another family in the area in the form of clothing and food.

Mr Sanyika also revealed that the household received grain from the government but he does not have to pay back the maize since he has a letter from the Department of Social Welfare. He said that he is often sick and that Tinashe takes care of the adults when they are sick. Mr Sanyika was observed on several occasions collecting food left in school children's plates at the boarding school so that they can eat at home.

This case shows that especially in the rural areas there are mechanisms to take care of orphans after the death of their parents. Most people in Biriwiri had no knowledge of child-headed households as children were left with guardians to take care of them. Nevertheless, orphans often have to contribute significantly to their own livelihood.

An impoverished family

The case of Laina illustrates the way children within the poor households were allocated tasks when parents became sick. It also shows the problems caused by a lack of economic resources and shortage of labour. Laina is sixteen years old, the oldest girl in the Dotito family. She is in Grade 7. Her father is a peasant farmer and he stays with his wife and seven children. Mr Dotito was retrenched from a manufacturing company in Harare during the first phase of the Economic Structural Adjustment Programme. He derives some income from building huts or houses for people in Biriwiri, but such contracts are rare. He also sells maize.

According to Laina, her work is important in the household because her mother is asthmatic and is often sick. During the time of study, Mrs Dotito was a patient in one of the mission hospitals. Laina had to do most of the chores, including looking after younger siblings. She was observed on a Wednesday and a Saturday.

Laina: Wednesday

Time	Task	Hours Spent
4.30 a.m. – 7.00 a.m.	Fetches water Cleans the house Prepares the fire and cooks Helps in preparing the younger children for school	2 hours 30 minutes
7.30 a.m. – 1.00 p.m.	School	
2.30 p.m. – 6.00 p.m.	Collects firewood Weeding in the field Cooking	3 hours 30 minutes
		6 hours

Laina: Saturday

Time	Task	Hours Spent
5.00 a.m. – 9.30 a.m.	Cleans the house Sweeps the yard Prepares the fire and cooks Fetches water	4 hours 30 minutes
9.30 a.m. – 12.30 p.m.	Weeding in the field	3 hours
2.00 p.m. – 5.45 p.m.	Washing plates Collects firewood Fetches water	3 hours 45 minutes
6.00 p.m. – 7.00 p.m.	Cooking	1 hour
		12 hours 15 minutes

Working week approximately 44 hours

She says she has no time to read or concentrate on her studies. 'I will be exhausted from the work that I can hardly read, for me I have to be like a mother when my mother is sick.' Laina also helps take care of her grandmother, who is too old to do any work. She says that she has too much work and can hardly cope but that she has to do the work to ensure the survival of the household. Laina allocates work to her siblings but usually it is the father who gives them the chores.

Laina explained that life is difficult for them but that the children had their labour to offer. This helped to sustain the household. She said that she had no hope of passing her exams because she hardly has time to read and study (the previous term she was positioned 35th in a class of 41). She attributes her poor performance to her work within the household.

Laina is not involved in any form of waged labour. She used to do piecework but stopped because her labour is mostly wanted at home. She said that since her father was retrenched, life has been difficult. Her father cannot afford to hire any labour. The family does not have a consistent cash flow. Most of the family's income came from Mr Dotito's other children from his first marriage, Mr Dotito's rare building contracts, and through selling maize. Laina said, 'We have to work hard as children to supplement the limited resources of the household.' This case shows that the work roles allocated to children are necessary for the livelihood of the family. Consequently children's work within the family or community goes unquestioned.

Kinship obligations

The Mirawo family moved as a group to Biriwiri in the 1970s from the Chipinge District. Mr Mirawo worked in a bakery in Mutare until it closed in 1992. Now the family lives off the land. The extended family in Biriwiri include Mr Mirawo's parents, his three brothers and their wives and children. Takura is sixteen years old and he is the second-born in the family. He is in Form 3 at Makwe Secondary School.

Mr and Mrs Mirawo have six children, three boys and three girls. The couple does not know the ages of their children and could only remember their grades. The first-born is a girl who had finished Form 4 the previous year. The second was in Form 3, the third Form 1, the fourth Grade 6 and the fifth Grade 4. The last child attended the crèche.

Takura viewed his role in the family as important. His main tasks are to help in ploughing, weeding and harvesting. He also fetches firewood and helps in building huts. He explained that he helps his relatives. For Takura, his father's brothers are also his fathers and so when they send him on an errand, he obeys. There are some tasks that the men do all together. For example, when it is time to prepare the fields for planting, all the men co-operate and rotate around each other's fields, Takura taking part. He also does some household chores like sweeping, cooking and washing clothes. Takura says the family faces different hardships especially a lack of resources. This increases the workload as the relatives try to work together for the survival of the family.

Takura explained that he sometimes does piecework for farmers or on the mission gardens. He also sells firewood for between $10 and $15 a bundle. He does not use the money to buy things for himself, but it contributes to his school fees.

Takura said that he hardly has time to rest or play. This is because Takura's relatives also make demands on him. These relatives include his father's father and mother, his father's two brothers and their families, and his father's sister and her children. Takura was observed for two days, a Wednesday and a Saturday.

Takura: Wednesday

Time	Task	Hours Spent
5.30 a.m. – 7.00 a.m.	Fetches water (for his household and for grandmother)	1 hour 30 minutes
7.30 a.m. – 1.00 p.m.	School	
2.20 p.m. – 5.50 p.m.	Weeding the field	3 hours 30 minutes
		5 hours

Takura: Saturday

Time	Task	Hours Spent
5.00 a.m. – 11.00 a.m.	Weeding the field	6 hours
1.40 p.m. – 4.00 p.m.	Gathering firewood (for his household and for grandmother)	2 hours 20 minutes
4.45 p.m. – 5.30 p.m.	Fetching water	45 minutes
		9 hours 5 minutes

Working week approximately 35 hours

Takura hoped to pass his 'O' levels at school, get a good job and be able to help his parents. He said he has problems in raising the money for his school fees. Other problems are lack of clothing and school stationery. Life is hard for children like himself, who have to work hard to help their parents, who are themselves hard-working.

His parents explained that there was no form of help for the children from the government. The Mirawos obtained grain from the grain loaning scheme because their granary caught fire and was burnt. They were supposed to be given ten kilogrammes of grain per person or child per month, that is, 80 kilogrammes for the whole family. In practice, deliveries of this amount only came roughly once every three months. Mr Mirawo said that maize loans were a problem, 'It increases our hardships because you have to struggle to return the grain and then after you have to get more grain loans.' On obligations to the extended family, the Mirawo parents said that since they were staying in a homestead full of other kin, their children were obliged to help. Mrs Mirawo said, 'You know these are not our own children, they are also children to our relatives, they can send them.' The Mirawo children help to collect water for their grandmother and they help their uncles also. For Mr Mirawo, 'Children work for their relatives because they are our kin and they cannot say "no". It is part of our culture.'

On how the children cope with a heavy workload, the parents said that the children rested sometimes but usually they compelled the children to work, especially in the field, because there were labour shortages. The Mirawos used to be involved in an income-generating project making hats, bags and mats but they stopped because they had no market for their products. They could not take their products to the Biriwiri craft centre because certain local people had a monopoly over the centre and it was difficult to become members, especially if you were poor and could not afford to pay the membership fees. Mrs Mirawo taught her children different skills and crafts, such as knitting, especially during the month of August when there was not much agricultural work. The parents and relatives valued their children's work, especially the grandparents, who could no longer do much for themselves.

Children who are not poor

Of a different nature is the work of children in the case of children who have parents who have more money. The study focused on how the roles of children differ in these families in terms of roles, coping strategies and welfare.

Princess is the third of four children. She is nine years old and in Grade 5. Her mother, Mrs Matewo, has been a widow since 1995. She trained as a family planning officer and has worked in various clinics. She owns a four-bedroomed house in Biriwiri. She used to operate some shops but had no business interests at the time of the study. Other children in the household are Tapiwa, who is twelve years old, Zororo aged ten and Joseph aged two.

Princess explained that children are important because they help parents in doing their chores especially doing fieldwork and selling fruits. Princess washes the plates, shines the floor, makes tea for her mother and helps in collecting firewood or weeding in the garden. Princess said that she would want to have more access to stationary for her schoolwork. She said that when she does not want to work she refuses or goes to play or read. During the time of the study it was observed that Princess sometimes refused to do the chores that her mother gave her like cleaning the bedrooms or weeding the garden.

Princess hopes to be a lawyer. Asked how her life was different from other children at school, Princess said, 'Some of these children come with no food to eat during break time while I have, some do not have clothing like jerseys and I have, they face different problems.' She also pointed out that children from poor families had various problems. She said, 'Some do not have shoes, so do not have uniforms or jerseys even in winter, they do not have fees and they are usually chased from school.'

Princess was observed for one day. She worked for approximately 1 hour 15 minutes.

Mrs Matewo explained that although she had a maid she still allocated chores to her children, 'We do it so that the children can learn the chores for their future lives and also so that they can stay healthy.' She added that her children had obligations to their kin. When the family visited relatives during the holidays, the children were given household chores to do. She said that her children are sometimes unhappy about doing their choresMrs. Usually they rest or play or read their books to avoid being given tasks. She added that they have time to play and usually they play for as long as they want.

Parental perspectives

Mrs Matewo explained that children were viewed as important in the Biriwiri community because they helped in tasks like collecting firewood, going to the fields, grinding mill and shops, and doing the laundry by the river. She commented, 'I see children doing these chores on their own without the help of the elders or adults and usually these children are aged between thirteen years and seventeen years old.'

Mr and Mrs Maushe commented on the importance of children in society. For Mr Maushe, 'A child is a vessel or an object which is good and better than any other object.' The general view was that traditionally children were the responsibility of parents alone but now, as children grow older, there are more caregivers like the schoolteachers, government, clinics and other people in the community.

Mr Maushe echoed the common view that many of their problems can be blamed on the Economic Structural Adjustment Programme: 'This ESAP is killing us and our families.' He explained that traditionally children were supposed to be looked after. 'Children need more care than ever because of the hard times we are experiencing. With the harsh economic climate…children are also faced with many problems and hence they need all the care.' He pointed out that there are orphans in Biriwiri, but that there were no child-headed households because their relatives took these orphans in. 'Relatives really play a big role in the upbringing of orphans,' he said.

While adults are supposed to care for children, children are seen as a prop to the households. Mr Sanyika commented, 'The child is your leg – the one you can send around.'

According to Mr Dotito, children are important because they are helpful in the household. He said that for example in female-headed households, children usually help run the household. He explained that children in most families are allocated different chores because of labour shortages. He said that he did not hire labour because 'there is no money in the household and we can rarely afford to hire labour.' Children had to fill in the gaps. According to Mr Maushe, children's work is very important in the household because they perform various tasks that the adults would not be able to do efficiently and effectively on their own.

Mrs Mirawo explained that children were important and were good for the household because of the work that they did. The common belief was that children were an asset. A family without children was seen as lacking or bad. Barren couples were shunned. She explained that she knew some couples who had remained childless for a long time and were viewed as social outcasts until the women finally conceived. The priority for all married couples was to have children, if possible in the first year of marriage. Mr Mirawo said that children faced difficulties in doing the various chores. He said that, for example, working in the fields was hard but most children did not complain. The distance to the source of water was also far (3.5 kilometres). Mrs Maushe commented that the children complain when we send them 'but they do not know that by making them work we are giving them wealth for tomorrow.' She explained that children are not rewarded for the work that they do because 'we will be working for our food'.

Mrs Mirawo commented that people often do not pay children well in waged labour. This discourages children from taking part in contract work.

When Mr Dotito was asked if the children work before they go to school, he replied, 'They have to work before going to school so that I also do not have a lot of work to do while they are away.' This suggests that adults impose chores sometimes for their own convenience rather than out of necessity. The children rarely complain, but simply followi their parents' instructions.

In Biriwiri work is seen as an important vehicle for conveying knowledge about one's community and environment. The study found that parents believed that work taught children to be responsible and to appreciate the value of things and the effort required to obtain them. The underlying concept seems to be that all family members are economic providers and that work prepares children for assuming adult roles. Mr Maushe said that culturally children were not to be lazy and idle but hard-working, thereby equipping themselves with skills for adulthood. Hence it was the duty of the parents to allocate roles to their children as part of the socialization process. Mr Dotito said with a smile, 'The children do everything including harvesting and even moulding bricks: that's what they are there for. The work that we give them makes them really work hard.'

On education, Mr Mirawo explained that his and other children in Biriwiri did not receive any help from the Department of Social Welfare, which refused to pay their school fees. This was one of the major problems for the children. Mr Dotito also emphasized this problem,

> You know we are stranded, we do not have cash, we do not know, we just send them to school and write letters to the headmaster for a grace period. But if we cannot afford the children will have to drop out of school. You know it's better to buy mealie meal than taking a child to school and then starve.

School officials confirmed the problem of fees for children from poor families. These children had constantly to be sent away from school because of arrears in school fees. Another problem was school uniforms. Most children came to school wearing whatever clothes they had and school officials had stopped insisting on uniforms because so many parents could not afford them. On grades, the school officials pointed out that some of the students from poor households performed well and others performed below standard. Even if poverty and children's heavy workloads contributed to low performance, these were not the only factors affecting children's academic performance.

Mr Dotito said that there was no programme in place to cater for the children's welfare needs. He pointed out that there had been a feeding scheme in Biriwiri about two years previously. Children were grouped into sections according to their place of residence and then children from one section went to one house where they were fed. The feeding scheme was funded by a foreign NGO and rotated from one house to another. It was very important for the children because it supplemented what the parents could afford to provide. Mr Dotito said, 'Now children are not very healthy but are weak.'

On health, Mr Dotito said that the children went to the local clinic when they were sick. They usually walk to the clinic or go by bus if the money is available. An interview with a clinic official revealed some of the problems that children faced, including malnutrition, diarrhoea, sores, measles, bilharzia, malaria and influenza. She noted that it was usually children form poor households that were prone to these health problems, and that the lack of resources impinges on the welfare of the children.

Conclusion

The chores performed by these children are not unusual in Zimbabwe. What is unusual is the time they spend working. Most work between 35 and 40 hours a week when they are also attending school. The working week is likely to be longer during school vacations in the peak agricultural season and much shorter during the agricultural off-season. The working hours of the children in this study are comparable to the working hours of the three per cent of children in paid employment.[14] Nevertheless, the work we have been describing in Biriwiri is more relaxed than formal employment, and children are allowed to rest when tired or when the weather is bad, unlike on commercial estates.

The study suggests that the most pressing reason for children's work is to meet the labour needs of households. We have seen that children's work is essential

---

[14] M. F. C. Bourdillon, 'Child labour and education: A case study from south-eastern Zimbabwe', *Journal of Social Development in Africa*, Vol. 15, No. 2, 2000a, pp. 5-32.

to meet the domestic and agricultural needs of several households. They help in cleaning, fetching water, gathering firewood, cooking, baby-sitting, working in the fields, watching crops and harvesting. Children as young as five help their parents by tending small animals, as well as participating in off-farm activities. As they grow older, these children assume other tasks during planting and reaping. Upon adolescence, they take on work that is differentiated according to gender. Boys perform tasks that require greater physical strength while girls concentrate more on household work and less on activities related to production. The number of hours that teenagers work is substantial.

Reynolds[15] points out, 'In many rural areas a girl aged twelve is no longer in command of her time...Child labour is vital to women.' This is true not only for girls but also for most children in the rural areas, who are allocated tasks as soon as they are able to work. This is highlighted by the case of the twins, who at the age of six had tasks allocated to them. Children's time is managed and controlled by their parents. During the time of the study, it was rare to see a child playing unencumbered by chores.

Besides work within the household, children work to raise essential cash, particularly for school fees. Although this study focused on children's work that is undertaken within the context of family, some children worked outside the family as hired labourers. Catherine, Tinashe, Laina, Gregory and Takura were all engaged in contract work at one time or another. Tinashe worked at a local tea and coffee plantation during the school holidays and at weekends as a picker. These children said that the money they earned was not used by themselves, but by their parents, mainly to supplement school fees.

Families use the contributions from children's labour to meet current needs and establish links among kin and neighbours to enhance future security. The workload expected of any particular child varied according to age, season, and the family's domestic cycle and in relation to the current social norms and economic realities.

Illness also contributes to the allocation of chores to children. We have seen that Laina had the major responsibility of taking care of her mother who was asthmatic. Tinashe takes care of his ailing uncle, who is his guardian, and his elderly grandfather, who is bedridden. As children share much unpaid domestic

---

15   P. Reynolds, *Dance Civet Cat: Child Labour in the Zambezi Valley*, Zed Books, London, 1991, p. xxviii.

work, they easily assume the role of carer when a member of the household, particularly an adult guardian, falls sick. Although such roles take up much time and energy, they are often invisible and not seen as real work.

Children need to work, and the work that they do is considered to be an important aspect of their training. The role of children within rural households is shaped by ideologies that serve the interest of the parents and the society. Most parents allocated chores or roles to their children as part of the socialization process whereby they believe they must equip their children with skills for adult life. It was felt that children should not be lazy and idle but should play an active role within the household. We notice that children from the well-off family were also given tasks as part of their socialization, but where there was no necessity there was little compulsion and the children often found ways of avoiding their tasks.

Work was also allocated according to gender. Girls were mainly involved in non-paid domestic work in the family home, while boys were more often involved in agricultural production and part-time contract work in agriculture. Catherine and Laina's tasks mainly centred on the domestic sphere whereas Matthew, Gregory and Takura worked mainly in the agriculture and outside the home. However, in some cases the issue of gender tended to be overlooked in the face of necessity. Tinashe had to do all the chores as he was the only child in the household.

Reynolds[16] points out that kinship ties are very important for children, who make considerable effort to nurture them. Children develop strategies to ensure co-operation and assistance among their kin. Families form the greatest means of support. Key informants indicated the strong socio-cultural expectation that the extended family should care for its members. The domestic group that regulates children's activities is not just the immediate family. In the rural setting in which most working children live, kin living nearby also play significant roles. On top of their daily routines in and around the home, children have kinship obligations. This applies particularly to orphans, who have to rely on their kin for shelter and protection. Tinashe has to offer his labour to his father's brother and his grandfather, with whom he lives. Takura has to perform certain daily chores for his kinsmen.

Children spoke of the most pressing problems that faced them. They complained of working for long hours and sometimes in harsh conditions. They commented that they hardly rested during the planting and harvesting season. The children would spend from three to five hours in agricultural-related tasks.

---

[16]   Ibid., p. 128.

Gregory and Takura commented that they suffered from exhaustion. Catherine said that sometimes her nose bled due to the heat when working in the fields. Some children carry out work that is dangerous for their health. For example, Tinashe complained that occasionally he had fallen from the ladder when picking coffee but did not complain or seek treatment even when he experienced a lot of pain.

Another common problem was the issue of hunger. Nearly all the children interviewed who came from impoverished families complained of having to work on empty stomachs.

In Biriwiri, the schoolwork of children from some of the impoverished families suffered. Children complained that they had no time to read. Gregory and Catherine acknowledged that they had no books to read at home. Even if they had had access to books, they had no time to read. Tinashe and Takura also attributed their failure at school to their heavy workload. Several studies have shown how work interferes with school performance in developed countries.[17] These suggest that more than fifteen to twenty hours of work per week can adversely affect a child's academic performance, by interfering with schoolwork and frustrating the teachers. Children in Biriwiri work well in excess of such hours. On the other hand, the education of poor children is sometimes hindered by their lack of school fees, and work can partly overcome this problem.

The work of children is seldom an individual strategy; rather, it occurs within the framework of the economy and is carried out in a variety of ways. These case studies demonstrate that children in poor families play a crucial role in the survival of the household. But child work is influenced by cultural factors as well as by poverty. Work is seen as an important vehicle for conveying knowledge about one's community and society and for learning responsibility. All family members must be economic providers and work prepares children for assuming adult roles.

---

[17] Jocelyn Boyden, 'The relationship between education and child work', Innocenti Occasional Papers, No. 9, UNICEF, 1994, pp. 33-35.

Chapter 3

Land, Women and Sugar in Chipiwa

Rekopantswe Mate

Department of Sociology, University of Zimbabwe

The Chipiwa Sugar Out-Grower Scheme in south-eastern Zimbabwe placed farmers on profitable irrigated plots for the cultivation of cane. This context required new interpretations of roles and initiated struggles for resources within households. The livelihoods of women and children were prejudiced by their lack of legal entitlement to land, which was vested in a single owner. This chapter explores these issues and places them in the context of land reform in Zimbabwe.

Since independence in 1980, land redistribution policies have favoured economically disadvantaged sections of the population.[1] Debate on land distribution has focused on the needs of different groups: blacks versus whites, large-scale versus small-scale farmers and lately the need to give land to commercial farm workers.[2] Within the different groups, the need for gender dimensions of land redistribution has not been highlighted.[3] Although some NGOs have been concerned with women's empowerment and land rights, they have been unable to substantially influence land reform.

This chapter criticizes land reform policies that assume households are beneficiaries. It pays attention to the political economy of households by looking

---

1 S. Moyo, *The Land Question*, Sapes Trust, Harare, 1995a.
2 S. Moyo, et al., 'The political economy of land acquisition and redistribution in Zimbabwe 1990-1999', *Journal of Southern African Studies*, Vol. 26, No. 1, 2000.
3 S. Moyo, 'A gendered perspective of the land question', *Southern African Feminist Review*, Vol. 1, No. 1, 1995b, p. 1. See also R. B. Gaidzanwa, 'Land, the economic empowerment of women: A gendered analysis', *Southern African Feminist Review*, Vol. 1, No. 1, 1995, pp. 1-12; and S. Jacobs, 'Zimbabwe, state, class and gendered models of land resettlement', in K. L. Staudt and J. L. Parpart, (eds), *Patriarchy and Class: African Women in the Home and the Workplace*, Westview Press, Boulder (Colorado), 1989.

at the cultural beliefs, norms and practices that prevail, and how these affect the flow of benefits from the returns of agriculture. The study also comments on the problems of land privatisation.

Research methods

Semi-structured interviews were used, together with observations in respondents' homes. The author personally conducted all interviews from 1998 to the end of 1999.

Availability of farmers was low. Many male heads of households were said to have acquired more and bigger plots in Chisuma, some 50 kilometres east of Chipiwa. The profitability of these ventures was not very clear. Estate officials said that these ventures competed with sugar production in terms of supervision and resources. Most men were present in cane-cutting season, when they spent much time in the plots supervising cutting, and when the level of activity is not conducive for interviews.

In the absence of men, women often declined to talk about sugar production saying that *'zvinoda varidzi vazvo'* (these things need the owners). I was therefore forced to use a sample based on availability. I formally interviewed 41 plot-holders, and gathered information on four more. Of the 41, 22 had inherited plots and nineteen were the original settlers. Twenty-two of the respondents were from monogamous households. In eighteen households the settler had more than one wife. One respondent was the only original female settler.

A brief history of Chipiwa

Mkwasine Estate, a private company, established the Chipiwa Sugar Out-Grower Scheme (also called the Chipiwa Mill Group)[4] in 1981 with government approval.[5] Mkwasine Estate is part of Hippo Valley Estates (Private) Limited, a large farming concern in the semi-arid south-east of Zimbabwe, producing citrus fruit, sugar,

---

[4]   This is for purposes of sugar milling quotas allocated to different sugar growing concerns or groups of farmers.
[5]   This information comes from an unpublished presentation by R. Mhungu, a settlement manager, in 1995.

beef and ethanol. The estates also produce animal feeds, mill maize and have a sizeable retailing concern.[6]

When Mkwasine was established, the colonial government, which had invested heavily in irrigation development by building dams, insisted that foreign-owned companies share irrigation water with private individuals.[7] Forty per cent of the water for Mkwasine Estate and 50 per cent of the water for Hippo Valley Estate was to be allocated to individual commercial farmers.[8] Prior to independence, white Rhodesians, white South Africans and Mauritians settled as out-growers with land holdings ranging from 100 to 300 hectares in size.

Chipiwa was born out of these circumstances in 1981, a year into independence. According to informants, the scheme was established hurriedly. Applications were invited through adverts in the media and in the local community. According to my informants, people were enticed to apply because of lack of interest in the scheme. A total of 192 farmers were settled. Farmers had an average of ten hectares of irrigable land under sugar cane. By early 2000, none had dropped out of the scheme.

Mkwasine Estate made a commitment to develop the land to be used by the settlers by supplying equipment and infrastructure for irrigation, surveying the land, partitioning the plots, taking care of administrative matters of the scheme, etc. The Estate provides facilities for water sources, overnight water storage and an overhead irrigation system. The Estate established a Settlement Office with a Settlement Manager[9], paid by the Estate, who oversaw all farming and administrative matters at Chipiwa, working in liaison with an administrator and an accountant. In addition, Chipiwa farmers can access other professionals employed by the Estate through personal relations and networks.

The settlers each received a residential stand with a basic, unplastered, two-roomed house of cement blocks, which farmers were encouraged to develop as they saw fit. Most farmers produce enough maize and a variety of vegetables to feed their families from the residential plots. Both the garden and the house were

---

6   A. S. Mlambo and E. S. Pangeti, *The Political Economy of the Sugar Industry*, University of Zimbabwe
     Publications, Harare, 1996, p. 34.
7   Ibid., p. 41.
8   Ibid., p. 40.
9   The estate abolished the post of Settlement Manager in 1998 amid complaints by settlers that it
     constituted some hidden costs to them. They wanted to be independent from the estate. The other
     posts remain.

fenced with mesh wire supplied by the Estate. The settlers were expected to pay the Estate $20,000 over fifteen years for the land before getting title deeds. At the time of study, no one had yet received title deeds.[10]

Chipiwa has a milling agreement with Hippo Valley Estates, which owns the only sugar mill in the country. Sugar cane is a bulky crop, which cannot be transported long distances cheaply and without deterioration. The mill is situated within 100 kilometres of the Estate and Chipiwa. A railway line runs through the Estate and carries cut cane to the mill.

After milling, statements are sent to the Estate with details of the source of the cane, sucrose content in the cane, price per unit, the total sucrose obtained per load of cane, total amount of money due to the farmer, etc. The accountant and his staff then pay the farmers after deducting expenses for labour, water and electricity, payments to the Estate for the land, loans to the Agribank, income tax and payments to other financiers where applicable. Some farmers have expressed distrust of the Estate management and its heavy involvement in running their affairs. They say that they do not understand some of the expenses they pay for and suspect that the Estate takes the money. Some ask what the Estate, as a business enterprise, stands to benefit by 'assisting' the settlers so much. Others question purported differences in sugar content of cane from adjacent plots and cane from the Estate.

Social characteristics of settlers

All but three original settlers are male and were married when they settled in Chipiwa. Most of their wives are not employed outside the home. A few women work as teachers and assistant nurses.

Of the three women settlers, one is a single mother, whose father is also a settler at Chipiwa. Another is a married woman who according to my informants is battered by her husband who wants to take charge of the plot. The third woman is a front for someone who already has another plot on the scheme: she was not present when I tried to visit her on several occasions and it is not clear how she benefits from the arrangement. Other women who have plots registered in their

---

10   I understand from personal communication with officials in the Ministry of Lands and Agriculture that they are working on giving title deeds to paid-up farmers through Mkwasine Estates.

names are widows who are running the plots for their sons or who have been able to inherit the plots from their deceased husbands.

Estate officials say that they did not discriminate against women when allocating plots. They say that they advertised and gave plots on the basis of a raffle after short-listing 'qualified' candidates. Inheritance is a family matter handled by the family and the courts. The Estate intervenes only marginally.

Most settlers were previously in unskilled and semi-skilled work in the Estate and in neighbouring communal farming areas. Few had more than primary education and very few have 'O' levels.

The settlers had no prior training in commercial agriculture or business and financial management. The Chipiwa settlers said that they had 'ample' knowledge and experience prior to settlement since they produced sugar cane for the Estate. Nonetheless, the Zimbabwe Cane Planters' Association, of which Chipiwa settlers are paying members, trained the settlers in all matters of sugar production after settlement. The Association also helps to inspect the crop for diseases because, if left untreated, contagious diseases might spread to other farms.

Finance for farming is obtained from Agribank and other financiers, with the assistance of the Estate. Some headstrong farmers go it alone. Because sugar cane is not harvested monthly, farmers do not receive an income on a regular basis. Good financial management is essential and training in this area is important.

The formation of co-operatives

Generally, farmers harvest over 100 tons per hectare, and as much as 125.1 tons per hectare in a good year such as 1982.[11] After the drought of 1991-92 farmers were left smarting from a poor harvest and low incomes. According to Estate records, Chipiwa farmers harvested 3.5 tons per hectare, compared to 1.9 tons per hectare on the Estate. Despite these adversities, financiers wanted money owed to them. Because the farmers had obtained loans as a group, Chipiwa Mill Group as a whole had to pay. Some farmers felt that those who work hard were subsidizing the sluggish ones. It was agreed that there was need to form co-operatives. Within these smaller groupings, people could motivate each other to work and it would

---

[11]   My colleague, Dr Emmanuel Manzungu, collated these statistics.

be easier to discuss issues of mutual concern and to make decisions. Eight co-operatives, varying in size from five to 48 people, were formed.

The co-operatives procure inputs and equipment, and mobilize labour. They organize cane cutting and loading, water distribution, road maintenance (both in the plots and residential areas), grass cutting and mending of perimeter fences. Roads are especially important as they allow tractors access to fields for farming, ferrying cut cane to train loading zones and the delivery of inputs such as fertilisers. Co-operatives also provide social amenities for farmers, such as the ubiquitous beer halls, which are patronised by men. There are facilities for women (social clubs) and for children (playgrounds). Co-operatives also ensure capital development where needed, such as enhanced irrigation facilities.

Elected officials, predominantly male, run the co-operatives. These officials have now become intermediaries between the farmers, Mkwasine Estate and other parties. Some co-operatives have offices and sheds to store co-operative equipment such as tractors and irrigation pipes.

Land ownership and its use

Land in the Chipiwa settlement is under private ownership. Farmers can use the land as collateral. Although the Estate does not encourage leasing of plots, this happens occasionally. Outright sale of the land creates problems in the absence of title deeds.

The residential stand can support crops such as maize, vegetables, sweet potatoes, legumes, banana, mangoes and papaya, and small livestock. Many households produce enough maize for consumption, but few, if any, produce surplus for sale. Women control this production and many men scoff at the income potential of such ventures. Many male settlers were at pains to say that they were capable of 'looking after their families' so there was no need for their wives to be seen selling fruit and vegetables at markets and bus stops. (Wives and children of Estate workers often sell fruit and vegetables at various points on the Estate, mostly along the main road with travellers as the target clientele.)

Many male respondents said that they saw sugar production as the major source of income in Chipiwa. Although land in Chipiwa is given to households for the benefit of the whole household, registered plot-holders do not normally discuss sugar cane business with other members of their families. Wives and children know that they depend on sugar production, but are not trained in any formal way on how to run their household plot. The registered plot-holder makes all decisions and attends all meetings. Some men portrayed sugar farming as very demanding and too sophisticated for their wives. In many male-headed households, women said they did not know much about sugar production (although it is possible that they claimed ignorance to me because they did not feel free to divulge information on sugar production in the absence of their husbands or sons).

The male-biased control of information and resources renders other household members vulnerable. Registered owners of the land can mortgage the land or otherwise dispose of it without consulting other household members. If it is true that women do not feel at liberty to divulge information, this too points to the gender basis of power relations within households which the policy of resettlement seem unable to address. This begs the question: who really benefits from land reform? Does the household as a whole benefit or only individuals within the household?

In one case, a plot was auctioned after a settler used it as collateral for a debt. He was unable to service the debt. The financier went to court and the Estate was unable do anything to stop the auction of the plot. At the time of doing research, it was said that the case had attracted government interest and the general reaction was alarm.

In a second case, the Estate was alerted early of a settler's non-repayment of a loan. The Estate agreed to see that the settler repaid the loan.

A third case involves a dispute over inheritance. The couple was childless and, according to common custom, was given a boy to look after by the man's young brother.[12] When the man died, his brothers forbade the widow from inheriting the plot and gave it to the deceased's 'son' instead. Initially, it seems the widow went along with the arrangement but changed her mind later. She suspected that the young man had no obligation to her since his uncle was now deceased. She had very little support from her husband's family in her bid to inherit the plot. She now lives elsewhere, leaving the young boy in charge. He lives on the plot with his young wife. He has the support of the Settlement office, which says that it is ideal that plots stay 'in the family'. Mkwasine Estate officials say that the young man is trying to run the plot properly and that productivity is in fact improving. They have suggested that the widow come to

---

12 Because the widow no longer lives on the plot, I could not hear her side of the story. The young man referred to her as his mother and to the deceased as his father. He also said that his uncles were in support of his inheritance. My informants say the 'uncles' in reality include his father.

stay on the plot in order to benefit from it. However, the boy's foster mother has sold the plot to someone else for $300,000 (US$7,895). She has already received the money from the intending buyer who now wants the plot. The case is still pending.

Male-biased access to information is evident in female-headed households. Widows often have to share information with sons who are minors, whether they are in charge on behalf of their sons or in their own right. Widows do not feel that they have irrevocable ownership rights legally and socially. Those interviewed said that they passed on all information to their sons because the plots were ultimately theirs. Where widows had inherited in their own right, they often felt that the male children had a right to know how 'their father's property' was being managed. For this reason, many widows called their sons to sit in on the interviews for this study. In male-headed households with original settlers, the men did not make an effort to ask other members of the household to be present at the interview.

Gender relations, marriage and effects of male biased access to information

The effects of lack of information and knowledge were revealed in those households where the original settlers are deceased and the widows had to be in charge.

In one case a widow of Malawian origin (as was her husband) did not know the amount of fertilisers she needed for her plot. She relied on her male neighbour, whom she referred to as her 'son-in-law', for help. She checked with this neighbour – who is not her son-in-law – before agreeing to be interviewed. The neighbour quizzed me a little and then gave his consent. The neighbour also reads and translates productivity statements for this woman.

In another case, an elderly widow, whose eldest son passed away a year after her husband, asked her husband's friend to manage the plot for her. The elderly man is single, and illiterate like the widow. The widow's second son is irresponsible and deemed unfit to manage the plot. The widow told me, *'pamba pane munhurume pane chiremera'* (a home with a man has respect). The elderly man lives with this family but does not seem to be well informed about sugar production. The deceased settler had two other wives who prefer the elderly man to be in charge. Since they live away from the plot, it was not possible to establish whether, as rumours claimed, these women were in control. The family resident in Chipiwa lives in a shabby house. This is also one of the households without a car: the car was sold when the heir fell ill a year after his father's illness and funeral.

Lack of information often mystifies the productivity of the plot. It does not allow for a smooth transition in managing the plot from one generation to the next. Sons who inherit often get the impression that their fathers have a lot of money even when they are in debt. In addition, plot-holders seem to feel that they should have 'an easy life'. This entails going away in the car, collecting money and deciding how it is to be spent while delegating work to hired workers. Meanwhile these workers cannot be bothered to do the work properly in the absence of the plot-holders. For instance, workers do not check the moisture level on the ground in the centre of the plot because in high temperature and humidity it can be very unpleasant in the middle of a cane field.

In polygynous households, women compete for their husband's favour in order to get more information than their competitors on how much money the plot brings in. In one case of sororal polygyny, the younger sister told me that she could see now – six months after her sister died – how the money was spent. Even before her sister died, she had insisted to the husband that 'no woman did groceries for her'. She went shopping with the man. Beyond ensuring that her two young children's needs were met, she could not decide on other expenses. According to informants, she controls the man more than her elder sister did. She is known to follow him to pubs and shout at him in public if he stays there till late. In another case, a 30-year-old woman previously married to her father's sister's husband, who already had three other wives, said that some of the wives used witchcraft to obtain favours from the husband. She got frustrated and left.

Many women do not know how much their husbands earn from the sugar or other ventures. When asked how much money was earned from the plot, many women simply said, '*Yakawanda*' or, '*[Mari] iripo hayo*' (It is a lot of money). The women tended to lament that the money had a lot of uses so it did not go far. Some said, '*Zvema*-settler *hazvizivikanwe*' (You just never know with these settlers).

It seems that any woman who spends time with the man of the house is likely to have access to more money for groceries and other immediate needs than women who do not. In addition, one can become privy to information on the man's finances. However, many men spend a lot of time away from home or hanging out with 'the boys'. Women who consider themselves to be 'decently' married would not spend time with men in bars. This puts younger wives and girlfriends at an advantage.

One strategy for a woman to spend more time with a man may be to get other women banished to the communal areas and move in with the farmer at his Chipiwa home. Another strategy is to ensure that he operates from where the woman is living. Some new wives insist on staying at their own places, so the farmers have homes in Chiredzi town, which is twenty kilometres from the Chipiwa. Others stay away but manage income-generating projects such as shops in the communal areas. These women stay well-informed about the ventures they are responsible for. Such information is strategic for married women when their husbands die because they can get their sons to inherit the ventures that are their responsibility or the ones they know most about.

Most women expressed anxiety over marital security because of the high propensity for polygyny in Chipiwa. Married women generally complain of multiple marriages. They see single women (including other farmers' daughters) as a threat to their marriages but feel that they cannot do anything to stop men marrying more wives.

Women resident in Chipiwa do not visit each other and therefore do not hear details of other women's experiences of marriage. Visiting other women at their homes is associated with gossip and brings disrepute to their families. Some women meet at church, but there are many churches and few fellow settlers' wives belong to the same church. There is great ethnic diversity amongst the people in Chipiwa, and some women are against taking advice from people of other backgrounds. There is a feeling that women from certain areas of Zimbabwe are 'less cultured' and therefore they are not likely to give good advice. As a result, women are socially isolated and most content themselves with staying at home tending the garden and supervising children.

Because most co-operatives have beer halls where men and their grown sons meet over drinks till late at night, men network better than women do. Control of information is closely linked to the ownership and control of land. In Chipiwa, when sons inherit, they continue to withhold information from others in the family. It is assumed that other members, once 'taken care of', have no business knowing anything about plot management. This monopoly of information allows the owners to make unilateral decisions about the disposal of the land and the use of resources from the plot.

Polygyny and the utilization of resources

When I started fieldwork in 1998, 26 per cent of the farmers were publicly polygynous. There are also informal polygynous marriages, where there are children, regular contact between partners, long-term relationships and expectations of dependence similar to those found in formal marriages. Some men had six wives and numerous mistresses. This led to a higher than usual number of children fathered by one man. There are many households with ten or more children.

It has been argued that polygyny is a form of labour recruitment especially in labour intensive production processes such as commercial farming.[13] However, in this study hired labour was prevalent and not family labour. Polygyny does however provide management for different enterprises.

A second argument put forward by Cheater[14] in her study of Msengezi is that polygyny is 'an idiom of accumulation'. Men marry more than one wife as a way of saying that they are wealthy. Multiple marriages point to the ability to pay bridewealth and to maintain numerous wives and children. This argument seems to best fit the case of Chipiwa.

Women also sometimes favour polygynous relationships. Some women want to marry a 'well-to-do' man, even when he is already married. In some cases, the woman's family thinks that one of their sons-in-law is wealthy and offer him another daughter as a wife. Thus we see the legitimization of sororal polygyny, which still takes place at Chipiwa. Multiple marriages provide a way of redistributing wealth. As indicated earlier, wives take charge of a portion of a farmer's investment portfolio when the farmer dies, whether this is a shop in a rural area, a house in Chiredzi, or resources from the sugar cane plot.

In some cases, sororal polygyny results because first wives prefer kin such as sisters or brothers' daughters as co-wives. In some cases, female relatives come to live with their married female kin to assist them with childcare and other domestic work. Sometimes a couple will bring in relatives and care for them, especially if the couple has no children.

---

13 See A. K. H. Weinrich, *African Marriage in Zimbabwe*, Mambo Press, Gweru, 1982, pp. 139, 143; A. P. Cheater, *Idioms of Accumulation*, Mambo Press, Gweru, 1986; S. J. Tambiah, 'Bridewealth and dowry revisited: The position of women in Sub-Saharan Africa and North India', *Current Anthropology*, Vol. 30, No. 4, 1989, p. 418.

14 A. P. Cheater, *Idioms of Accumulation*, Mambo Press, Gweru, 1986.

There is an often-held view that the first wife can control co-wives who are related to her, unlike non-kin. This was not seen to be the case in Chipiwa, where female kin married to the same man were observed to fight bitterly. This was exemplified in the two cases of sororal polygyny that I came across. In one case, the older sister was infertile, putting her at a disadvantage. In another case the older sister had only one child. The younger sister, who has two children with the man and is expecting a third, accused her older sister of witchcraft and trying to kill their husband who no longer loves her. She says this is why their husband is sickly. The older sister has since left the plot leaving the younger sister as the woman of the house.

In the absence of education and skills that would permit women to be economically independent, marriage becomes the most viable source of sustenance. In one case, two young co-wives married to a man who is no older than 25, said that as long as the man could buy them food, clothes and shelter they would stay with him without complaining. They said that it was pointless for women to fight each other because men are uncontrollable. If a man cares for all his wives and is fair to them, then women have to co-exist, the two said. These young women have no other means to a decent life. One of them worked as a storekeeper in a rural store before she was married. She says that her life is better now than it was before. The two women keep each other company when their husband is away, as he often is. They both agree that ordinarily it is hard to tell whether a man is married or not because men do not always tell the truth about their marital status. Sometimes polygyny is a rude surprise both for married women and new wives.

It is clear that the women's lack of economic power lands them in polygyny. They get married to polygynous husbands for their economic survival, and then fight with the other wives for their respective sons' inheritances.

In polygynous households, women become the focus of the mobilization of resources for their children.[15] The order of marriages determines the seniority of children and their chances of inheritance. A woman and her children are seen as a distinct unit. Women compete with each other, and co-operation between children of different wives is rare. Since plots cannot be subdivided, inheritance becomes a 'winner-take-all' affair, The children who do not inherit and their mothers are immediately impoverished if they have no alternative sources of sustenance. Even

---

15   R. S. Oboler, 'The household property complex in African social organization', *Africa*, Vol. 64, No. 3, 1994.

where there is co-operation, mutual suspicion tends to be high and the co-operation does not last. The evidence from Chipiwa suggests that polygyny can compromise livelihoods in the long run, although it benefits men contracting these marriages.

Access to moveable property

The vast majority of settlers have vehicles. Most of them have pick-up trucks, which were bought in 1994-95 with finance from up-market financiers. Most of the vehicles are still on hire purchase agreements, although few farmers would admit to it. Some farmers have had their vehicles repossessed by financiers (but later returned) because they were unable to service their debts. None of the men interviewed admitted to the fact that their vehicles had been repossessed. One widow admitted that her vehicle was repossessed when her late husband's brother, who had inherited her, was siphoning money to other ventures for his other family.

The person in whose name the plot is registered generally uses the vehicle at his discretion. Consequently, one finds that men predominantly drive the vehicles. This also accounts for men's high mobility and frequent absences from home.

Male mobility is a source of insecurity for a lot of married women. As the women themselves note, farmers generally travel after they have been paid. Many wives worry that other women will be brought in as wives when the farmers get back. Women do not think that they can stop men from absenting themselves.

One woman said that when a settler is away from home for days on end, it is almost certain that he is with a girlfriend or a new wife. Often men have informal wives or mistresses. These girlfriends sometimes have children with the men and expect to be maintained. A number of male settlers have ventures such as shops in the communal areas, which their mistresses look after. Wives may or may not know of the other women, and many do not get any benefit from these ventures. They know that if their husband should die, the girlfriends or mistresses looking after any other of his ventures will simply appropriate whatever is in their care.

Ensuring that one's children are well catered for is a sensible investment because children are expected to look after their mother if their father dies, or their parents become estranged. If a man is able to look after his children (feed them and pay their school fees) many women are fairly content. This is why when a woman leaves her husband she leaves the children behind in the hope that they will be looked after. However, children whose mothers are absent have limited chances of proper care and education, and are unlikely to inherit the plot. In the interest of their children's welfare, women are better off staying on the plot unless they have alternative means of survival.

Use of income

All respondents indicated that they make a living primarily from farming sugar cane. Few respondents openly declared that they have plots in Chisuma[16] or that they have plots elsewhere. When asked about other income-generating projects, many suspected that I was from the income tax office and were not forthcoming. The following table shows average incomes from sugar cane, for the various co-operatives.

Table 2: Average earnings and expenses per co-operative in 1999.

Name of co-operative*	Number of members	Average income (Z$)	Average expenses (Z$)	Net Income (Z$)**
Pump 42	6	823,226	175,888	647,338
Section L	37	184,857	3,615	181,241
Kudzanai	20	1,050,660	517,322	533,338
Porepore	47***	815,635	230,146	585,489
Phases 3 and 4	37	662,518	310,983	351,535
Phase 2	21	682,149	185,927	496,221
Pump 4	5	758,665	162,446	596,219

* Data missing Section metres co-operative.
** The exchange rate was US$1=Z$38 in 1999.
*** Data available for 47 members although altogether there are 48.

Average expenses include all that are documented by the administrator's office. They include income tax, loan repayments, payments for utilities such as water, irrigation facilities, electricity, road maintenance, labour, use of tractors and other equipment, as well as other expenses accruing because of co-operatives' developmental initiatives. From the net income farmers also have to plan for the

---

16   Chisuma is about 30 kilometres to the east. Many settlers have been granted plots there by chiefs, where they produce rain-fed maize and cotton to augment their income.

next season if they do not wish to rely on loans (although many said that this was inevitable). At individual household level, school fees of children, health care, vehicle maintenance and kinship obligations are key financial concerns. Most farm and off-farm needs have skyrocketed in price lately due to inflation, and many farmers complain that their pieces of land are 'too small' for their needs.

In view of the fact that most household expenses were not documented, I focus my attention on children's education, which even without documentation is more easily quantifiable. I also take education as a key intergenerational investment for farmers. I also think that it is used as an indicator of social progress. Many women defined children's education as a key need, one that ensures their own long-term survival.

Children's education

Children's education is a major expense all over Zimbabwe. In Chipiwa, as in the rest of the country, the head of the household is expected to pay school fees. Currently declining employment rates and an inflation of qualifications mean that education is no guarantee of a job. Nevertheless, education remains the best possibility of upward mobility and poverty alleviation, sometimes through employment outside the country. Consequently, many parents in Zimbabwe try to send their children to school.

In the close to twenty years of Chipiwa's existence, only a handful of settlers have been able to give their children professional training, in spite of the relatively high incomes of these farmers. Of the 41 respondents, eighteen have no children with tertiary education, even though they have children in their late teens and older. A few had up to five children with tertiary education. Of the 41 respondents, 27 have no working children despite post-secondary school training. This is because many did courses such as dressmaking, tailoring, knitting and typing, sometimes with less reputable institutions. The children remain dependent on the plot.

Some settlers lamented this state of affairs, saying that they would have liked their children, especially boys, to go to school and be gainfully employed. It is said that the children feel that their parents are wealthy without any schooling, and see school as a waste of time. Dropout rates are high because of lack of fees or truancy. Some settlers say that as uneducated parents they cannot set good examples of the advantages of education. When children look at their parents in comparison with local professionals such as teachers and nurses, their parents look to be better off because they have cars, live in better houses and earn more money per year. Although this is true, the plots are unlikely to provide for the many children in the same way.

It is taken for granted that girls will get married. Due to the predominance of virilocal post-marital residence, it is expected that their husbands will look after them. For this reason, girls do not qualify for inheritance. Increasingly, some daughters are beginning to question why they, as children of the deceased, do not inherit like their brothers. They say that there are no guarantees that they will get married and stay married. Many say that since they are not educated and cannot get jobs elsewhere they too need access to plot proceeds once their fathers die. Some widows sympathize with their daughters but they cannot do anything about it. At the time of research, no daughter had legally challenged the *status quo*.

One can argue that education is not only an investment but also some a form of pre-mortem inheritance, which a man can give his children. It lessens the intensity of inheritance squabbles among surviving children by giving the children options for sustenance. However, the wealth of Chipiwa has not spilt over to the children as much as one would have expected and descendants are likely to be poorer than their settler fathers are.

Transmission of land within households and between generations

Although the laws of the country uphold equality between the sexes, the persisting legal duality renders this impossible because African women can be discriminated against for cultural reasons. The transmission of land seems to follow cultural ideals, which in reality are inappropriate for immoveable property.[17]

Most women in Chipiwa do not have information about their rights as widows. All meetings are organized through the co-operative structures, at times in liaison

---

[17]　Similar problems have been noted in Kenya. See A. P. Okeyo, 'Daughters of the lake and rivers: Colonization and land rights of Luo women', in M. Ettiene and E. Leacock (eds), *Women and Colonization: An Anthropological Perspective*, Praeger, New York, 1980; F. Mackenzie, 'Land and territory: The interface between two systems of land tenure, Murang'a District, Kenya', *Africa*, Vol. 59, No. 1, 1989, pp. 91-109; M. Silberschmidt, ' "Women forget that men are the masters": Gender antagonism and socio-economic change in Kisii District, Kenya', Nordic Africa Institute, Uppsala, 1999.

with the Estate. These are all male-controlled institutions. It is therefore difficult to educate women of their rights on any subject. Talking about the rights of widowhood raises suspicion and is seen as *kufurira* (bad education). Women are therefore in the dark when their husbands die and do not know how to go about winding up estates. In any case, widows do not wind up their husbands' estates alone: custom requires that they do so with their husbands' relatives. Men on their part do not leave wills. Inheritance by a son is preferred even when precedents show that many sons do not run the plots properly after they inherit.

Inheritance is usually decided a few months after burial to enable the farming enterprise to continue and to allow the surviving family access to money in the deceased's bank accounts. The process involves the courts, the family, and the Estate. The co-operatives play a peripheral part as advisers. Most people go to the magistrate's courts in Chiredzi while some go there via the family courts and community courts.

Of the 41 respondents in this study, 22 (54 per cent) were from households in which the original settler was dead. In most of them, sons have inherited or widows have inherited in trust for their sons. There are three widows and one daughter who have inherited in their own right.

According to the prevailing understanding of customary law, women cannot own property independently of their husbands.[18] In addition, they have contractual incapacity and consequently have to be accompanied to the High Court and elsewhere when winding up the estates. Ncube[19] echoes this sentiment when he says that under customary practices a woman is 'an unpaid servant of her husband'.

Customary law is also founded on kinship ideology, according to which only members of a kin group can inherit from each other. Since spouses belong to different kin groups, they cannot inherit from each other. These ideologies worked well in the past when people accumulated property within the kin group or through the assistance of other members of the kin group. Now kin groups have been replaced by the nuclear family as the group within which production and consumption take place. In the minds of officials however, when there is a dispute, the larger kin group takes precedence. People do not consider their spouses their closest kin even when they have lived with them for years.

---

18 T. W. Bennett, *Human Rights and African Customary Law*, Juta and Co., Cape Town, 1995.
19 W. Ncube, *Family Law in Zimbabwe*, Legal Resources Foundation, Harare, 1989, p. 17.

In patrilineal societies where marriage is exogamous and post-marital residence virilocal, wives do not qualify to inherit from husbands. It is feared that once women inherit land, it might later be inherited by their kin and pass to an alien lineage. Daughters do not inherit for fear that their husbands might take the land. However, the dispossession of women as wives and daughters and their resulting pauperisation raise a number of questions when people see how young male heirs mismanage the plots and income from them. The resulting dissonance between the ideal and the reality in Chipiwa may lead to debates that will enable policy change. We have seen a case in which a widow tried to sell her plot while her late husband's kin insisted that it be inherited by a fostered son. Here are some further illustrations of the problem:

A young man in his early 20s, with older sisters, inherited a plot after both his parents died. He was in his third year of secondary school, but then dropped out. He used to drive without a licence and crashed his father's car, which is now a write-off. He would like to repair it but has spent all the savings that his parents left. The young man is frequently drunk and is unkempt. Many people refer to him as one of the worst examples of inheritance by a son. Some of his siblings are still at school but are often suspended because their fees are not paid on time. The plot is not well looked after because there is little supervision. He disappears for days after being paid. Mkwasine Estate officials, in collaboration with his co-operative, have agreed that money should be paid to his 24-year-old sister's account in the interest of the other children, although the young man is the registered plot-holder.

The second case is a friend of the first. He is also young, drinks a lot and is generally scruffy. His father had four wives: one died, two left him and one (the third wife) stayed. All women left their children (sixteen in total) to be cared for from resources from the plot. The third wife's son inherited the plot because his mother was resident. There is however tension in the family: the heir's half brother, a son of the first wife, is constantly challenging him for control of the plot's resources. According to informants, the third wife makes decisions for her drunken son although he implements them. The house was untidy inside and outside and there were a lot of badly dressed children in the yard.

A third young man, in his 20s and without 'O' levels, is very arrogant, stubborn and a bully. He has two young wives and three small children. He drove his mother and his father's second wife from the plot, saying that they were old and should go to the rural areas to be peasant farmers since their husband was dead. He told them that he would look after his father's children. The young man lives on the plot with his wives, children and siblings, but is rarely at home. The siblings looked miserable and some have dropped out school. He also drives without a licence but was recently arrested and made to do community work. His young wives boasted to me saying that 'settlers have a lot of money'. They do not mind their husband's long absences as long as he buys enough food and clothes for them and the children, and they have a roof over their heads.

In another case, a widow complained that at the end of 1998 her 23-year-old son withdrew $83,000 (US$2,200) from his father's estate and took his father's car for a pre-Christmas spending spree. He and two young friends were said to have stayed at the luxurious Mahenye Safari Lodge and at the Sheraton Hotel in Harare. He has spent three months away from home. He is rumoured to be living with a girlfriend somewhere, using the money left by his father. At the same time, a fifteen-year-old girl turned up at the widow's house eight months pregnant. The widow was bitter at having to look after the pregnant girl, but pretended to the public that the young girl was her daughter-in-law, protecting her son from prosecution for sex with an under-age girl. She did this even though the son stripped his father's estate and prejudiced the livelihood of other dependants. She did not think her son was fit to be heir. She was anxious to get hold of him and make arrangements so that she could be given full control of the estate or at least be co-signatory to all transactions.

A friend of the above is an heir who also went on the spending spree. He was still a minor, aged seventeen, when I visited. He dropped out of school after he threatened to assault one of his teachers with a knife. His mother runs the plot in consultation with him. When I interviewed her, she had him called saying that he was the one in charge. He listened to our discussion without saying much. I later heard that the young man is rowdy especially when in the company of his friends and under the influence of alcohol.

In a sixth case, an original settler had four wives and an estimated 30 or more children. The wives squabbled over inheritance and all four left the plot. The son who inherited the plot also left, but retains control of finances. The children who live there do not agree on how best to proceed. This was the only household that does not engage in horticultural production in the garden. Most of the children are now adults and live on the plot with their wives and children. No one works. Two of the brothers on the plot are former border jumpers who worked in South Africa for a while.

There are cases where women disinherited their sons because they felt that the inheritance of sons was unfair but in other cases it was because the sons were irresponsible.

One 41-year-old widow, whose husband died in 1996, said that she was unhappy with the decision to allow her thirteen-year-old son to inherit the plot. This decision was made at *mudzviti's* (District Commissioner) office, with the encouragement of her husband's relatives. She subsequently went to High Court to have the decision overturned. She maintains that the plot is for all her four children and she will see to it that their needs are met. What irked her most was that immediately after her husband's death, her thirteen-year-old son demanded to be informed of the affairs of the plot. Her husband's relatives had told him that this is 'his' property and that no one should interfere with him. The widow has since 'put her son in his place'. She says that he is well-behaved and going to boarding school. He drives the family car when he runs errands for his mother.

A 47-year-old widow, who is also a teacher at one of the local schools, said she had worked alongside her husband in the farming project. Her husband died in 1996. She inherited the plot and has been referred to as a trailblazer in mothers 'disinheriting' sons. Her son is a graduate and another child works in the banking sector. Both have good relations with their mother. Other children are in secondary and primary school.

In a case where the couple had only three daughters, the man is said to have fathered a number of children, including sons, out of wedlock. The man died suddenly of meningitis, and his brothers tried to inherit the widow but she declined. The relatives insisted that the daughters should not be given the plot, and that 'there were other children' who had to be brought to the hearings. There was no evidence that the 'other children' were fathered by the deceased. The widow accepted one son and obtained a birth certificate for him, but retained her eighteen-year-old daughter as the heir. Her husband's family claims that the woman killed her husband so she and her daughters could monopolize his wealth.

In another case, the original settler died in 1986 and his widow agreed to be inherited by her husband's brother, who was already married. She bore him one child. However, the man took the proceeds from the plot and built a store in the rural areas which was run by his first wife. The widow was unhappy with this. The man died in 1996 and she refused to be inherited again. She was expecting her fifth child at the time of doing research. She has inherited the plot in her own name and her in-laws do not bother her: they suspect that she has supernatural means of killing their sons in order to control the plot.

These examples show how young men inheriting their fathers' estates can be very reckless, and have rendered precarious the livelihoods of dependent family members. Siblings' education is disrupted because school fees are not paid. These heirs take family property for themselves.

Women's inheritance is contested on grounds of kinship ideologies. The women who eventually inherit are viewed with suspicion. Co-wives compete with each other to have their sons inherit. Where widows are evicted from the plot, there is no way of telling whether these women have access to income from sugar production or not. What is clear is that children's livelihoods are rendered precarious. Thus land privatization has created new forms of vulnerability while sharpening intra-household tensions. Households are sites for struggles over access to resources and not sites of harmonious resource sharing.

Discussion: Who benefits from land reform?

In answering this question, we question the assumption that members of the household benefit as a group from a commercial enterprise, given prevailing cultural norms in which farming ventures are not run like group ventures. The reality is that some members benefit more than others, while certain members, such as younger children and women, stand to lose, especially when the original settler dies. Struggles over access to resources are not acknowledged and addressed by policy makers.

Households as sites of contested access to production

There are two main perspectives on households. One, the 'moral economy' perspective,[20] sees households as harmonious units, in which resources are pooled and many activities shared. Often the household is seen as headed by one person, usually a man, under whom all resources are centralized and through whom all resources are distributed. The head of household is assumed to be inherently altruistic and to distribute resources to each according to need. Related to this view is the perspective that giving land to women disrupts family unity.[21]

In the moral economy perspective, household members are driven by social ideals about what should be done, when and how. This creates long-term interdependence as people are bound by obligations to one another. According to

[20] D. Cheal, 'Strategies of resource management in household economics: Moral economy or political economy?', in R. McC. Netting, R. Wilk and E. Arnould, *The Household Economy: Reconsidering the Domestic Mode of Production*, Westview Press, Boulder (Colorado), 1989, p. 12. See also, E. Fapohunda, 'The non-pooling household: A challenge to the theory', in D. Dwyer and J. Bruce (eds), *A Home Divided: Women and Income in the Third World*, Stanford University Press, Stanford, 1988.

[21] S. Jacobs, 'The gendered politics of land reforms: Three comparative studies', in V. Randall and G. Waylen (eds), *Gender Politics and the State*, Routledge, London, 1998.

Cheal,[22] relations are ritualized and have a sense of sacredness. People cannot easily deviate from these expectations and resource flows are taken for granted.

This view is attractive to many policy makers[23], partly because it escapes political issues within households. It also negates calls for equality between men and women by playing down women's insecurity. It ignores the fact that access for women to resources is connected to marriage or patronage, and that marital insecurity results in material insecurity.[24] We have seen that this view is prejudicial to women and children in Chipiwa.

The second perspective, which Cheal refers to as 'the political economy of households', is that households comprise people bound together by relations of authority and dependence, based on prevailing cultural norms and values. Co-operation is not guaranteed. It emphasizes self-interest of members and power differences, which enable some members to mobilize the productive and reproductive labour of others. Those members whose labour is mobilized have a limited say in how household resources are used. This ensures their continued dependence on those with resources. Relations between people are transactional and punctuated with negotiation, bargaining or open conflict. Power relations determine resource flows, whether they emanate from socio-cultural values or material endowment. This view portrays better the state of households in Chipiwa.

Nevertheless, the ideology of kinship influences the terms of women's strategies to maintain access to resources for themselves and their children. As Cheal points out, in practice households are both moral and political economies.

Gender biases of focusing on the household

One of the salient features of this case study is that women are discriminated against in access to productive resources. Multiple marriages, numerous mistresses

---

[22] D. Cheal, op. cit., p. 14.

[23] See E. Fapohunda, op. cit. on land policies in Nigeria among the Yoruba; A. P. Okeyo, 'Daughters of the lake and rivers: Colonization and land rights of Luo women', in M. Ettiene and E. Leacock (eds), *Women and Colonization: An Anthropological Perspective*, Praeger, New York, 1980, pp. 186-213, for land policies among the Luo in Kenya; M. Silberschmidt, ' "Women forget that men are the masters": Gender antagonism and socio-economic change in Kisii District, Kenya', Nordic Africa Institute, Uppsala, 1999, on Kenya and S. Jacobs, 'Zimbabwe, state, class and gendered models of land resettlement', in K. L. Staudt and J. L. Parpart (eds), *Patriarchy and Class: African Women in the Home and the Workplace*, Westview Press, 1989 on Zimbabwe's land resettlement policy.

[24] M. Silberschmidt, op. cit., notes that in Kenya women's insecurities are on the increase despite a rise in rural productivity.

and children spread resources so thinly that the benefits to these individuals are very limited in the long term. We also see that it is because women are economically marginalized that they accept polygynous marriages, in which their long-term needs and those of their children are not guaranteed.

If women had been given land in their own right or allowed to control portions of the farm proceeds, the likelihood of benefits being more concentrated in a smaller groups of kin is higher. In my view, many children would have gone to school since many women expressed this desire.

In a study of African entrepreneurship, Wild[25] notes that family enterprises exist only in name. In practice, family businesses are often treated as the private property of one person, the entrepreneur, and subsequently his heirs. Although the African family is popularly viewed as united and harmonious, the family embodies relations of entitlement.[26] Some of the entitlement is based on envy and greed. Many who feel that their entitlements have not been well honoured pilfer from the enterprise if they can. In Chipiwa however, because the plots cannot be divided, heirs treat the enterprise as personal property and not a family concern, making it difficult for other dependants to benefit from the plots. This forces women into subservient, patron-client relations with men. The personalization of 'family property' negates the idea of group beneficiaries. The case of Chipiwa shows that male control of land also disrupts family unity.

Agarwal[27] notes that it is erroneous to assume that the land rights of women will somehow be fulfilled within these family or household models. She says that rights to land have to be definable and enforceable by some authority, whether these are usufruct or ownership rights. We have to ask what the discernible rights to land of women and children in each model of land reform are. Is there a way in which individuals who feel short-changed by their families can seek redress? Agarwal further notes[28] that in rural areas where economies are based on agriculture, access to land ensures a transformation in gender relations which is critical for real economic empowerment to occur. Improved access to production resources ensures better bargaining within marriage and within the community. Sen[29] echoes this

---

25   V. Wild *Profit Not for Profit's Sake*, Baobab Books, Harare, 1996.
26   Ibid., pp. 108-114.
27   B. Agarwal, 'Gender, property and rights: Bridging a critical gap in economic analysis and policy', in E. Kuiper, J. Sap *et al.*, (eds), *Out of the margin: Feminist perspectives on economics*, Routledge, London, 1995, p. 268.
28   Ibid., p. 281.
29   A. Sen, 'Varieties of deprivation: Comments on chapters by Pujol and Hutchinson', in E. Kuiper, J. Sap *et al.*, (eds), *Out of the Margin: Feminist Perspectives on Economics*, Routledge, London, 1995, p. 51.

sentiment when he says that 'material deprivation' and 'political disempowerment' are connected. Jacobs[30] points out that the assumed unity and relations of dependence in peasant households have to be problematized.

It is ironic that although economic empowerment is at the centre of current land redistribution debate,[31] gender dimensions of empowerment are at the periphery of the debate. Studies on women's experiences of life in household and intra-household dynamics are rarely acknowledged in policy debates, where models of household unity and harmony have led to the further marginalization of women.

---

[30] S. Jacobs, 'The gendered politics of land reforms: Three comparative studies', in V. Randall and G. Waylen (eds), *Gender Politics and the State*, Routledge, London, 1998.

[31] S. Moyo, 'The political economy of land acquisition and redistribution in Zimbabwe 1990-1999', *Journal of Southern African Studies*, Vol. 26, No. 1, 2000.

Chapter 4

Women in the Bark-Fibre Craft in Biriwiri

Paradzayi Pathias Bongo

Department of Sociology, University of Zimbabwe

Bark-fibre craft is a significant element in the livelihoods of many women in Biriwiri. This chapter illustrates conflicting interests and interpretations both within the community and between members of the community and officials, resulting in different perceptions of what is required for the preservation of the environment. We also find negotiation and conflicts between the craftworkers, arising in part from the ways in which they organize themselves.

I collected the data in Biriwiri Ward, Chimanimani District in south-eastern Zimbabwe from September 1998 to August 1999, mainly through participant observation and unstructured interviews with selected craftworkers, merchants, professionals and operators of curio and craft shops in Harare, Chimanimani and Mutare.

The research sought to examine environmental conservation and rural livelihoods as an arena of conflict. Focus was on different actors, their perceptions of trees and how these in turn affect soil loss or conservation as they engage in their livelihoods. I have narrowed down my focus to a longitudinal study of Biriwiri women engaging in tree bark-fibre craft. Other actors in natural resource use in Biriwiri include the Department of Natural Resources (DNR), professionals like officials from AGRITEX (Department of Agricultural Extension), non-governmental organizations (NGOs), Chimanimani District Council, the Forestry Commission, animators and other 'outsiders' as well as grassroots leadership (headmen, chiefs, councillors, village development committees, etc.).

The women use the fibre of *miombo* tree species, *Brachystegia glaucescens* (*muunze*), *Brachystegia speciformis* (*msasa*) and *Brachystegia boehmii* (*mupfuti*), to make artefacts like dolls, mats, blankets, bags and even clothes. The women do not perceive their crafts as damaging to trees and to the environment. Instead they shift the blame for deforestation on traders in firewood and on those who mould bricks for sale, as well as on the increasing population which forces people to clear marginal land for agricultural purposes.

Biriwiri is a sub-catchment named after the Biriwiri River that flows through it. It forms part of the Nyanyadzi sub-catchment and is very mountainous, reaching from 870 metres where the Biriwiri flows into the Nyanyadzi River to 1,957 metres at the highest point in the catchment, with very steep slopes. The variation in altitude results in differences in the rainfall received and temperatures experienced in different parts of the area under study. The downstream parts are dry and hot, whereas the upstream parts are colder and wetter. The soils are mainly red with a lot of stony gravel. Since the area is so hilly, people have managed to cultivate crops on terraced patches of land as a soil conservation measure. The remaining area is for firewood and for grazing and construction purposes. Also included in this study are the neighbouring villages Nyamusundu and Saurombe, plus the western Mhakwe Ward.

Crops grown include millet, wheat (under irrigation), beans, maize, sunflowers and sorghum. At the time of the research there was an acute shortage of agricultural inputs, particularly fertilizer and seed and this drove up their prices. The majority of people in Biriwiri could not afford to engage in any meaningful large-scale crop production, owing largely to these exorbitant input prices. Further, the steep slopes characterizing the terrain of the area make crop farming very difficult as most crops run the risk of being washed away by surface run-off water. During the 1998-99 agricultural season, fertilizer was too expensive and scarce. Some unscrupulous middlemen and shop owners measured out small packets from 50kg fertilizer bags. They then resold these small packs of about two kilograms or more. In some instances, one 50kg bag could fetch $700-750[1] for a businessman through this trade. This would be too exorbitant for the farmers, considering that the normal price for one 50kg bag of ammonium nitrate was then $289.

---

[1]   At the time of research one US$1 was equivalent to approximately Z$40.

Environmental debates

The study has been carried out in the context of how best to achieve environment-friendly modes of livelihood in an age where environmentalism has become prominent. Environmentalism impinges on public consciousness through many channels: press reports and television documentaries; government policy statements; pressure group campaigns, commercial advertising and charity appeals. Sometimes it appears as a preservationist, conservative influence,[2] sometimes as a radical challenge to established political and economic principles, and at other times as a spiritualist vision.

Agreement about the identification of environmental problems is not universal. The following however are widely accepted: pollution, diminishing natural resources, the increasing size of the human population, the destruction of wildlife and wilderness, losses of cultivable land through erosion and the growth of deserts, and the endangering of the life-support systems of the planet. Milton[3] says that the perception and understanding of environmental problems and their possible solutions have shifted over the years.

Significant disagreement emanates over the fact that there is not a common understanding of what constitutes an environmental problem. Problems are sometimes understood, as by Attfield,[4] as intolerable costs to humans which human action can eliminate or at least alleviate, with a principal concern for humans alive now. Another view takes into account the next 50 or 100 years, or perhaps longer. People with this view are likely to be satisfied with solutions that effectively safeguard the interests of those humans on whom they focus their attention. This is akin to Davis'[5] diagnosis:

If you want your new baby ever to be able to fish in the streams, you had better join in the fight for clean water now.

There is also a pragmatic view according to which there is actual or possible harm to living organisms in general. Here some extend their concern to the welfare of sentient animals, others to the interests of all living organisms, while yet others

---

2   S. Cotgrove, 'Environmentalism and Utopia', *Sociological Review*, Vol. 24, 1976, p. 24.
3   K. Milton (ed.), *Environmentalism: The View from Anthropology*, Routledge, London and New York, 1995.
4   R. Attfield, *The Ethics of Environmental Concern*, Basil Blackwell, Oxford, 1983, p. 1.
5   W. Davis, 'The Land Must Live', in K. S. Shrader-Frechette (ed.), *Environmental Ethics*, Boxwood Press, California, 1981, p. 85.

concentrate on species, ecosystems or the biosphere as a whole. In some cases, non-human interests are given precedence over human interests in general by the 'deep greens/ecologists', as illustrated by Wayne Davis:

> *All living things are created equal and are interdependent upon one another. All flesh is grass. Only plants can make food. Man and all other animals are totally dependent upon the plants which we so casually put aside in pursuit of the ever greater megalopolis.* [6]

The extreme position presents humanity as a cancerous growth upon nature, and the human species as constituting the problem. Holders of these conceptions are less satisfied with human-centred solutions, and particularly ones confined to the short-term future.

Different views of what makes a problem reflect not only different estimates of possibilities, likelihood and the limits of tolerance, but also disagreements about moral principles and about what is of value in itself. Eco-alarmism has taken a very prominent place within today's environmental discourse. Mol and Spaargaren[7] draw attention to the emerging field of risk theory, which reflects upon the identification, perception and management of risks. Focus now seems to be on distribution of high-consequence environmental risks rooted in the process of globalization. High-consequence risks are risks that are remote from control by individual agents, but threaten the lives of millions of people and even humanity as a whole. The impacts of environmental degradation are always socially and spatially differentiated. They may end up affecting the global environment, but first they damage small parts of it. These local effects frequently transgress national boundaries: acid rain from England damages Danish and Norwegian forests; water pollution from Switzerland destroys the ecology of the Rhine in Germany, etc.

In this study, politics are about environmental decisions and the various policies and ideologies concerning the use of natural resources that affect decisions to use trees and their products. They are about who decides how to harvest trees, and about whose definition of degradation counts. They also concern the epistemological terms of reference in advocacy and formulating and effecting policy, for instance on intervention in natural resource utilization. With reference to the

---

[6]   W. Davis, 'The Land Must Live', in K. S. Shrader-Frechette (ed.), *Environmental Ethics*, Boxwood Press, California, 1981, p. 89.

[7]   G. Spaargaren, and A. P. J. Mol, 'Environment, modernity and the risk society: The Apocalyptic Horizon of Environmental Reform,' *International Sociology*, Vol. 8, No. 4, 1993, p. 431.

women's craft co-operatives, the politics are also about how some women are excluded from craft co-operatives while members enjoy the benefits of being members of registered co-operatives. We are also concerned about how decisions are implemented and applied to the Biriwiri community. The elite professionals of DNR, various NGOs and the District Council, have come up with various decisions regarding tree use, including imposing fines on villagers caught felling trees. Related to this is the assumed superiority of official 'scientific' courses of action over the 'primitive' approaches adopted by the locals in Biriwiri, particularly women involved in the bark-fibre craft. We need to explore the implications on natural resource utilization, policy and practice, of the ways in which some types of knowledge dominate others.

Ethnographic history of bark-fibre craft

Before the advent of the woollen blanket (*gumbeze*), the traditional blankets were called *makudza*. These were woven, like the *nhembe* (short aprons worn by women) and the *mhapa* (used by men) from bark fibre. As imported cloths and home-made cloth were relatively difficult and expensive to obtain, most people used bark-fibre cloth. Only hunters and traders could acquire skins. One Portuguese chronicler of the sixteenth century noted how the people of Batonga (Shona-speaking people to the north) dressed in the bark of trees, of which they also made containers.[8] In the late nineteenth century the use of bark for the manufacture of many items was common among the Karanga of Masvingo province. Bark collecting occurred at a particular time of the year, and whole families would take part, making the activity a social occasion. Large quantities of material would be collected to make blankets and cloth, string, arrow quivers, beehives and granaries. A new-born Shona baby was wrapped in a *gudza* (pleated fibre blanket) dyed with red soil so that it still looked clean when a stool was removed.[9] Bark fibre was also used to make the *muputi*, the strip of string tied around the waist of a child.[10] The *chisvino* (a type of beer strainer) and the *domo* or *chifumbiro* (a muzzle to prevent cattle from munching the new crops), were made from strips of bark string or bark lath, as was the *dendere* (the covered-in cage for carrying fowls to market). The German explorer, Carl Mauch, relates hunting with *mampulas* (bark-

8   H. Ellert, *The Material Culture of Zimbabwe*, Harare, Longman, 1984, p. 90.
9   M. Gelfand, *Growing Up in Shona Society: From Birth to Marriage*, Mambo Press, Gweru, 1979, p. 4.
10 P. Berlyn, 'Some aspects of the material culture of the Shona people', NADA, Vol. 9, No. 5, 1968, p. 72.

fibre nets) in the Tokwe-Lomagundi area in 1871. Making bark-fibre nets was part of young boys' training for manhood. A young man might also weave a wig of fine bark fibre which, nicely knotted, he affixed to his hair. Tonga girls in the eastern chiefdoms of the Gwembe valley adopted a 'coming out' dress at puberty when the girl was given the skirt of *musanta* fibre.[11] When the girl went out of the homestead, she was required to don a veil composed of strings of baobab fibre. Young Tonga boys also put on a fibre fringe apron and loincloth. When hunting and herding cattle, men and boys would carry a knobkerrie, an axe and a *nhava* (a big bark-fibre bag).

The arrival of the whites in the nineteenth century brought modern cottonseed and commercial methods of production. In addition, it led to the large-scale production of cotton and other cloth. The result was that the production of traditional cloth, which had thrived perhaps for many centuries, was discouraged as happened generally in Africa. Compared to fast methods of modern production of cotton, the traditional methods suddenly appeared dauntingly difficult.

From utility to commercial art

Craftwork by women using tree fibre has been going on in Biriwiri since time immemorial. The great-grandparents of the current inhabitants used tree fibre to weave blankets in order to keep the family warm at night. The craftwork has come to be known generally as *magudza*. According to the early members of the women's craft co-operative at Muusha Rural Craft Centre in Biriwiri, a Mrs Chitombo from Mutoko exposed them to vigilant marketing of their craft items. With encouragement and support from Mrs Chitombo, these women divided themselves into groups with different specialities. Some specialized in making hats and others in making blankets. Mrs Chitombo took their artefacts for marketing in Harare. Some whites who saw the items were impressed and placed orders. This heralded the commercialization of Biriwiri women's craft, which was originally for local consumption only. Women are engaged in this craft throughout the whole year, even during the summer season when people are busy in the fields. However, fibre yield is low in the dry season, when the trees shed their leaves.

---

[11]   B. Reynolds, *The Material Culture of the Peoples of the Gwembe Valley – Kariba Studies*, Vol. 3, Manchester University Press, 1968, p. 206.

Organization of craft co-operatives

At the time of research, there were four craft co-operatives, namely Muusha craft co-operative, Shingirirai, Muzinda and Totonga village co-operatives. Only Muusha and Shingirirai are formally registered. Although there are different age groups involved in the craft, the middle-aged women (35-50 years) are dominant. A very insignificant number of men are involved directly in the craftwork.

Muusha was the biggest and most successful co-operative and has a building in Biriwiri. It has 65 members with a well-defined structure of command and offices: a chair-lady, a vice chair-lady, a secretary, a vice-secretary and a treasurer as well as committee members. This club was established around 1968. Members meet every Monday at 2.00 p.m. to work on new orders and to discuss any issues pertaining to their craft. Their shop is well stocked and they have employed a 32-year-old lady to sell their products. Normally, each woman specializes in different items, such as blankets, hats, dolls, mats, small animals, bags and even clothes.

Members contribute twenty per cent from the sales of their artefacts towards the co-operative. This money is used for stationery, building and licensing as well as paying the shop attendant. They also run a grocery section in the craft shop in order to cushion the co-operative in times of low activity in the craft business. Items in this section include mealie meal, dried fish, avocados, tomatoes, sugar, salt and cooking oil.

The Shingirirai craft co-operative is second to the Muusha co-operative. It was started in 1976 under auspices of the Catholic Development Association. It is situated 4.5 kilometres from the Muusha craft co-operative, and it has a membership of 58. The organizational structure is similar to that of the Muusha co-operative. Members meet every Wednesday. They display their artefacts in their shop, which is situated 30 metres from the tarred road. Besides selling tree fibre material, the co-operative also sells dyed cloth, at times with embroidery. The Catholic Development Association sometimes conducts workshops with the women on management of business, serving and general conservation issues, including campaigns to plant sisal. Members keep the money they get from selling craft items only to share it when the volume of sales is substantial.

The Muzinda co-operative is an emerging group, which is situated in Saurombe village, seven kilometres north-east of the Biriwiri business centre. It has 29 members who meet every Wednesday to distribute work on orders and also to build their craft shop, which is incomplete. They also engage in various fund-raising ventures to finance their building, especially contract agricultural work. About half of the women are widows who are trying to make ends meet through the craftwork. The Muzinda craft shop is situated somewhat remotely and cannot be seen from the main tarred road. The co-operative has the same organizational structure as the two established co-operatives.

The Totonga village co-operative comprises 36 members. These women have not yet elected a structure for their co-operative. This group, established in 1996, is distinct in the highly cohesive social relationships that were visible at the time of the research, reinforced by the strong Christian beliefs held by the members, many of whom belong to the Apostolic Faith Mission. The members also own and run a consolidated garden that supplies the Biriwiri clinic with vegetables, a deal they clinched in July 1999 orchestrated by a local AGRITEX officer.

In Nyamusundu village, eight kilometres east of Biriwiri, there is another co-operative, but it is riddled with organizational and viability problems owing to its remoteness. The co-operative is not yet registered and has about 30 members. There was talk of a cheque that had been supposed to be payment for craft items sold in 1997, which disappeared into thin air. This has been a major cause of dissension among the members, who no longer have faith in the whole co-operative nature of the craftwork. Some members have therefore left the co-operative to work alone.

Apart from members of the various co-operatives there are many women in Biriwiri who are doing the craftwork as individuals. This is because the established co-operatives are no longer accepting new members on the grounds that they are now over-subscribed. Fibre craft is the most common off-farm, economic activity in which Biriwiri women are involved.

Processing and marketing of artefacts

Few of the women in Biriwiri are involved in cutting and removing the bark from trees to make *ngoi*. In this system of specialization, the women in Mhakwe ward do the extraction of fibre and sell the *ngoi* to the women in Biriwiri, who weave it into goods for sale. To extract fibre, the women cut tender shoots of the young *miombo* trees. They also cut softer branches of mature trees of the same species. They extract the fibre mainly by beating the tree or branch with dry sticks to break the outer hardness leaving the fibres inside. They then boil the fibre together with ash for colouring. They dry the fibre and pound it with mortar and pestle. The fibre is pressed to soften it. After this, the fibre is spun into strands or strings (*ngoi*) of the desired length and thickness. The standard length of each *ngoi* is two metres. The strings are sold in bundles of twenty strings. One bundle of fibre cost $2 in September 1998. By August 1999 it had risen to between $3 and $4.

Weaving involves placing two sets of parallel fibres at right angles to each other and interlacing one set through the other. The warp is held taut while the weft is interwoven through it. The women also do tapestry on some of their artefacts. This is a special type of weaving in which the weft yarns are manipulated freely to form a pattern, or design on the front of the fabric.

The weavers sell their products to merchants or passing tourists. News about prices and quality requirements from other villagers may be the only source of information other than the trader. These kinds of horizontal linkages are important as a means of information sharing, to consolidate power in buying and selling, and to mobilize political support in lobbying for policy change.

There is not much variation in the pricing of artefacts in Biriwiri. The prices of mats vary with the size. A mat measuring 70 centimetres by 35 centimetres costs $75, one of 90 centimetres by 60 centimetres costs $85, and a mat 200 centimetres by 200 centimetres costs $800. Table-mats cost $30 to $35 per set of six. Bigger blankets can be converted into carpets and fetch higher prices of more than $1,000.

The craftwork is labour intensive. It takes approximately one week to weave a mat of 70 centimetres by 35 cm. A large mat takes a month and larger carpets as much as two months. It takes one to two days of part-time work to weave a set of table-mats. Hats take two to three days. The heavy demands on labour are not only in weaving but also in debarking and pounding fibre.

Most women maintain that the craftwork has empowered them economically. Some 60 per cent of the women have managed to educate their children through craftwork. Some children have even gone up to university level. Some women have bought cattle and upgraded their homes using the money they earned from the craft. Their earnings, though, have not been substantial of late, but they help out on vital goods like salt, sugar, and bread. The women engage in rational calculation of the opportunities and options available to them as viable sustainable livelihoods. One Mrs T had this to say:

Magudza are easier because we get the resources locally and therefore cheaply, whereas other projects like poultry would require us to source raw material elsewhere thereby becoming too costly and alien to us.

The women have indicated a general dwindling of marketing opportunities in craft items.[12] However, they still do not accept prices dictated to them by buyers, but haggle and negotiate over an amount they deem fair. I witnessed the sale of artefacts to a trader, Mr Mponda, in July 1999 in Totonga village at Mrs Mushanguri's home. Mponda and the twenty women had a heated negotiation over prices that went on for one and half hours before the former agreed to buy the products at a higher price than what he had offered at first. For instance, he wanted hats for $13 each, and the women wanted to sell them at $20 each. The two parties then agreed on a temporary price of $15 per hat. They cited the increasing costs of buying bundles of *ngoi,* which were now selling at $3 each. With a hat requiring four bundles, the women would end up spending $12 on *ngoi* and then get only one dollar as profit.

It's now like a casino... our husbands will now end up questioning where the money for the sale of artefacts is going.

It was said over the radio that if you used to give your mother $100, these days it is $10, therefore the prices of the hats and bags must increase.

In the light of the growing number of craftworkers, new and vigorous marketing strategies must be adopted by these women if they are to survive the stiff competition. There are also craftworkers in Birchenough Bridge, Chipinge, Nyanyadzi and Nyanga, who compete with Biriwiri women for international customers in the urban centres.

Main merchants and buyers of Biriwiri craft items

The National Handicraft Centre is one of the principle buyers of the artefacts. It was created in 1989 and it stocks sling bags, bark-fibre bags, mats and dolls from Biriwiri women. It started as a community development project under the then Ministry of Community Development and Women's Affairs. The Centre has a gallery

---

[12]   The following year, the market was further reduced by the large-scale collapse of the tourism industry following political unrest in the country.

n Harare, where they sell their goods and export them to Canada, Japan, Australia, France, UK, Austria and US. According to the manager, westerners are very keen to have goods that are hand made and the opposite holds for third world people. The Centre advertises the artefacts on their web site and sends catalogues to tourists who enquire about African hand-made goods they wish to buy. They are also in the International Directory of Resources for Artisans. There are some NGOs who work with National Handicraft Centre in promoting the artefacts within their home countries, for example OXFAM in the United Kingdom and Fair Trading or Alternative Organization in the Netherlands. At the time of the research, the artefacts coming from Biriwiri women to the Centre were getting less owing to the dwindling market opportunities for bark-fibre craft on the international market caused by too many bark producers, creating a glut of artefacts.

Another buyer is the Zimba Craft Co-operative in Harare. According to Mrs N, they came to know of Muusha women in the early 1980s. The items they took from Biriwiri included baskets and *gudza* items like bags and dolls, but they do not stock fibre mats. Tourists came to know of Zimba Craft through adverts placed in tourists' journals. Swift transport carries their orders from Biriwiri. Other products sold in Zimba Craft Co-operative include cloth, painted cloth or materials, painted boards and wire toys. According to her, tourists love *magudza* very much for their authenticity.

Besides organizations buying craft artefacts from Biriwiri, there are also a number of individuals who do so. Ms Y is a Japanese lady who has been buying the craft items from Biriwiri since 1982. She normally places her orders by phone and sometimes by writing to the co-ordinator, Mrs Muyambo. She makes the artefacts more appealing by specifying the measurements and also by instructing the women to use thinner strings. If the artefacts fall short of the prescribed measurements, she will not take them. Ms Y is the Muusha Craft Co-operative's most regular customer. For the period of 20 February 1998 to 1 November 1998, she bought goods worth $67,720, including square fibre bags, bucket bags, entrance mats, floor and table mats. In December 1998, she bought Christmas presents for members of the craft shop, perhaps an indication of high cordiality between them.

Ms M.J.G. of Chimanimani started her own craft shop around June 1996. She buys and stocks fibre items from Biriwiri for reselling to tourists. Items on display include bags, hats, tortoises and dolls, all made from bark fibre. She also stocks and sells other craft items like wire and metal toys, tie and dye clothing and wooden carvings. Women wishing to sell their bark-fibre products to the shop do so every Saturday. However, goods are subject to a strict selection criteria and competition. Some women walk away with $3,000 per sale or trip to the shop.

Mr Charles Mponda, based in Karoi (north of Harare), is perhaps the most dynamic of the buyers, though he buys mostly the products of Totonga village co-operative. His first response to my question for information was,

Any person to whom I explain my artefacts will end up buying them.

He began his business selling winnowing baskets from Honde valley, and started buying *magudza* on 27 July 1986. He said that he was supporting the women so that they have a market and their children benefit in the future. He resells the items to tourists in Kariba, Victoria Falls and South Africa. The tourists come from Germany, America, the UK, and other places. He has plans to set up markets in Kenya and other African countries. He pointed out that whites do not prefer sisal items, since sisal is an import from the West and they want full traditional material that is authentically African. Mr Muponda is currently preparing a fact sheet on the weaving of *magudza* from the first stage of harvesting tree fibre to that of weaving, so that buyers will be well informed and also as a way of advertising the craftwork on behalf of the women. He normally orders items worth $4,000-$5,000 per month. He takes around $7,000-$8,000 from their sale. He reinvests his takings in the craft business in order to generate more money. He claims this business has increased his circle of acquaintances and has given him social enhancement. Most of his clients, including tourists in Kariba and Victoria Falls, call him 'Schoolboy'. He says he earned this nickname because when he sells the craft items he explains thoroughly to his intended buyers, in the manner of a schoolboy answering a teacher's questions.

In his dealings with the women he sometimes adds an element of barter trade, whereby he exchanges their *magudza* for second-hand clothes, dried fish and belts. For instance, he traded two fibre bags for a single shirt after negotiating with one woman selling artefacts in Totonga village in July 1999. On the day in question he bought goods worth about $4,000 from the women.

Conflict on tree use

Many women in Biriwiri eke out a living through the craftwork described above. This mode of livelihood has been, or is being, perceived differently by various actors, some viewing it as detrimental to the environment and others viewing it as insignificant. All the women interviewed maintain that their use of trees in craftwork does not damage the trees. They argue that they have been taking the bark since time immemorial but the trees are always there and the craftwork is still thriving. As one said,

> *We have been doing this since long ago and the trees have not been wiped out.*

The chairlady of Shingirirai Co-operative, Mrs Madinya, had this to say about those people who accuse them of destroying trees:

> *We are saying they don't know what they are saying.*

To ensure that the trees they use in craftwork are conserved, the women say that they have taken it upon themselves to enforce some form of collective social responsibility on tree use, since trees are an important source of livelihood for them. There would be no rationality in using the trees in an unsustainable way, since they need to continue in the same livelihood for ages to come. Mrs Madinya showed me a baobab tree in her home yard as she stressed the point that she has been using that tree for fibre since she was a girl and it is still growing strong. The women are also aware of the fact that trees need to be conserved to protect topsoil from raindrop impact. One woman said,

> *We saw the trees we had cut shoot again year after year and we were convinced that we were not destroying trees.*

Social restraint sometimes guides people in their use of natural resources. There is a case on record in Mhakwe Ward illustrating just how strong this moral self-restraint is. People in the area know that they can be penalized for cutting down trees. Mr Muranda, the local DNR representative in Mhakwe, showed me a tree that had been cut by someone in late October 1998, who then became afraid to come and collect it. The person who had cut the tree was afraid of being detected, knowing he or she had flouted social norms governing tree preservation. The tree was still there in January 1999. In Mhakwe, the collective social responsibility is not confined to trees only but also to other natural resources. For instance, anyone caught by other villagers washing clothes in Mhakwe Dam is reported to the authorities, who will then take disciplinary action against such a person.

Of the men interviewed, about 60 per cent believed that bark-fibre craft is harmful to trees. They said that most of the trees that had been harvested would die. This would leave the soil exposed to the raindrop impact, thereby contributing to soil erosion, the men said. One 58-year-old man expressed concern about my identity when I was interviewing the women in Totonga village in July 1999. He thought that I was a detective who had come to seek information to be used fo suing the women. He appreciated the economic benefits of the craft, but he foresaw a situation whereby the craftwork would no longer be condoned due to the deforestation it is causing.

Some men support the craftwork. They assert that *magudza* is a sustainable venture in that people have been doing it for many years and the trees have survived. These people point to other factors. Chief of these is that trees are los as people cut them down for firewood or to clear land because of population pressure.

Similarly, chiefs and village heads, the traditional custodians of natura resources, voiced concern over the rate at which trees are dwindling, bu attributed it to factors other than the craftwork. Headman Muusha attribute deforestation in the area to people who cut trees for firewood and not fo craftwork. The leaders are supposed charge a fine of $150 per tree cut. There i: also some patrolling supposed to be done in the hills and forests by about ter men based in Mazvarirani village, who are meant to apprehend anyone felling a live tree. Firewood can only be collected from dead trees or can be bought at a nearby wattle tree plantation for $50 per standard trailer-load. This is more than most rural families can afford.

The local councillor, Mr Joseph Manangwe, said that no-one, not even the women, are allowed to cut trees, but because of poverty, people end up doing so About the craft, he said,

> The craftwork is very beneficial, we are yet to assess if it damages the environment..
> In fact, it is like thinning since every year the trees sprout again... It's our industry tha
> we survive on.

Mr Manangwe holds that cutting trees for craft could be ecologicall beneficial, creating spacing for the trees so that they have enough nutrients to grow. The representative of SAFIRE (Southern Alliance for Indigenous Resources in Chimanimani also mentioned the possible benefits of thinning. He said that SAFIRE could consider sponsoring the women in their craft, subject to a scientific assessment by their ecologist of the impact of the project on trees.

The politics of exclusion

Women who want to join established craft co-operatives can do so no longer because the co-operatives are over-subscribed. This amounts to conditions of enclosure whereby some people are excluded from participating in this potentially lucrative venture. It has become difficult even for women who weave good items to sell them if they are not affiliated to any one of the formally established co-operatives.

Such a condition of exclusion in natural resource use in Biriwiri has created a situation similar to conditions of the politics of enclosure highlighted by the Ecologist.[13] Enclosure has redefined the bark-fibre craft community and shifted the reference points by which people are valued. In such a situation, increasing numbers of people do not have access to the formal marketing channels, the political process of natural resource use, and the knowledge used. As has been observed in Biriwiri, enclosure ushers in a new political order. When the environment is turned over to new uses, a new set of rules and new forms of organization are required. At the end, old forms of environmental management and arrangement are forced into redundancy or vilified, derided or outlawed.

The Department of Natural Resources (DNR) has a mandate to promote tourism. I asked the local representative of DNR how the Department could reconcile promotion of rural tourism through the women's craft while at the same time maintaining that the women were contributing to environmental degradation. The DNR considers the women's craft as damaging to the environment, even though it does not have hard facts to prove their viewpoint. The District Head of the DNR, Mr Maziwisa, had this to say,

> *The methods the women employ in their craft are too primitive and we want to eradicate them, but this doesn't happen in a day...the people need to be educated on proper use of their resources.*

His view was that the DNR was not opposing rural tourism *per se*, but was pointing towards other resources, for example the water reed. Mr Maziwisa later said that people should get permits to engage in craftwork from the district council. The local authority should sanction the amount and types of tree species to be

---

13   The Ecologist, *Whose Common Future? Reclaiming the Commons*, Earthscan Publications, London, 1993.

used. He said that with permits the craftwork becomes easier to monitor and assess and also it would be possible to control the number of people involved at manageable and sustainable levels. Of the co-operatives, the Muusha and Shingirirai are formally registered and they pay dues to council. According to him these are allowed to operate because they contribute revenue to council of about $810 per year. He observed,

> When these people do it, they do not damage trees because they contribute to the local authority and the money they pay is used for the conservation of the same affected tree species.

The payments are however hardly significant contributions to conservation in the area. This is particularly critical when the ecological cost of harvesting these trees for craft is not known, as is the case in Biriwiri. Enclosure in another sense appears to have contributed to accelerated tree loss since some people and institutions have erected fences around what they claim to be their land. By so doing, they exclude others from the right to use trees on common land. The increasingly higher population densities have resulted in total land area (including trees) available for the commons diminishing thereby creating pressures in the remaining unfenced areas. This phenomenon is summarized in this remark by one of the male interviewees,

> There is the mission school, elsewhere are homes ... there is fence everywhere. There is nowhere to go.

Intervention in natural resource use[14]

The major player in intervention to date has been the DNR. The DNR is campaigning to make villagers use trees that replenish quickly for crafts, firewood, building poles and other things, instead of the *miombo* species used for bark fibre. The Department does not support the fibre craftworkers, particularly those who are not members of established and registered co-operatives. The district head of the DNR expressed the official position of his organization as being not sure whether the craftwork should be promoted or encouraged, because of its potentially

---

[14]   I have written at greater length on this subject in an article entitled, 'Intervention in natural resource use in Biriwiri', *Zambezia*, Vol. 28, No. 2, 2001, pp. 133-46.

damaging effect on trees. They have chosen to adopt the 'precautionary principle' in natural resource utilization, taking preventive action ahead of scientific certainty on the grounds of its being better to be safe than sorry.[15]

The DNR has intervened in natural resource utilization in Biriwiri and the Chimanimani District in a number of ways, the main ones being the establishment of animators and plantations, and the Mhakwe Dam project. Animators are people given training on environmental issues, who then go about the villages lobbying for sustainable use of natural resources. There are two animators in Biriwiri, who liaise with the DNR on issues pertaining to conservation such as policing stream bank cultivation and cutting down trees, and advise on the construction of terraces and digging contour ridges. However, they lack power and cannot enforce sanctions on offenders. People may thus choose to ignore them or to ostracize them should they be too diligent in carrying out their duties. One government official had this to say concerning the issue,

> *No one has real power… People fear each other. A lot of things are said on paper concerning environmental conservation but nothing materializes … Our government is very good at organizing and running seminars which produce no real follow-up and effectual implementation of policy recommendations from these seminars.*

The Mhakwe Dam project is a project of CAMPFIRE (Communal Areas Management Programme for Indigenous Resources), under the auspices of the Ministry of Water and DNR, and completed in 1994. Initially, this project was intended to allow those on the upper side of the dam to fish and those on the lower side to irrigate. The Mhakwe area animator is confident that it will be possible for them to divert Mhakwe women's attention from craftwork to commercial fishing. By 14 July 1999, there were workshops in Mhakwe on the by-laws to be used on the dam. The women however claim that they were not consulted about the project, and that they are not interested in fishing.

The DNR supports consolidated gardens near the dam, where villagers can earn a living through utilizing water from the dam. The women, as in Biriwiri, are also being encouraged to plant sisal for soil conservation and as a possible substitute for indigenous bark fibre.

---

[15]   J. Argent and T. O'Riordan, 'The North Sea', in J. X. Karperson *et al.*, *Regions at Risk: Comparisons of Threatened Environments*, United Nations University Press, New York, 1995, p. 391.

Discussion of research findings

Much has been said about the rural poor who engage in environmentally damaging activities, through so-called ignorance. In Biriwiri, professional beliefs about people and the environment need to be challenged. A number of issues arise from this research relevant to the controversy on how to balance conservation and the need for human survival.

While it is good to curb environmental degradation, Chambers[16] would want us to proceed with caution in intervention, especially as he asks, 'Whose reality counts?' He warns against regarding indigenous people's views as inferior. This, Chambers says, leads us as researchers and policy makers to 'box ourselves in'. One of the means by which policy makers 'box themselves in' is through labelling 'target groups' as passive objects of policy (e.g., 'the landless', 'sharecroppers', 'women'), rather than as active subjects with projects and agendas of their own. 'People, conceived as objects of policy, are defined in convenient images' and such classifications are 'represented as having universal legitimacy, as though they were in fact natural'.[17] Wood argues further that labels misrepresent the situation and reveal the relationship of power between the giver and the bearer of a label.[18] Labelling can legitimize the actions of development agencies and other public bodies.[19] In Biriwiri the professionals and authorities label the craftworkers as wrongdoers.

There is evidence that in many developing countries forests contribute significantly to food security, nutrition and medical needs, income generation and poverty alleviation. Given such a scenario, policy planners need to distinguish between conservation as preservation of existing biological capital and conservation as sustainable exploitation of resources – trees in this case.[20] When people sometimes need to exploit natural resources for their livelihood, conservation means efficient management of natural living resources so that the amount harvested is just as much as the rate of regeneration allows. It is highly unlikely that the economic

---

16 R. Chambers, *Whose Reality Counts? Putting the First Last,* Intermediate Technology Publications, 1997.
17 G. Wood (ed.), *Labelling in Development Policy,* Sage, London, 1985, pp. 1, 9.
18 G. Wood (ed.), *Labelling in Development Policy,* Sage, London, 1985, p. 11.
19 N. Long. and J. D. van der Ploeg, 'Demythologising planned intervention: An actor perspective', *Sociologia Ruralis,* Vol. 29, No. 3/4, 1989, pp. 226-250.
20 D. Brown, 'Participatory biodiversity conservation: Rethinking the strategy in low tourist potential areas of tropical Africa', Overseas Development Institute, No. 33, August 1998.

goals of local users will coincide with the conservation goals of those concerned with preserving biodiversity. Policy recommendations from extreme 'deep greens' would prevent people from utilizing natural resources. Milton highlights the fact that environmentalist arguments can be ill-founded and inconsistent. He adds,

Environmental discourse is essentially political, shaped by vested interests struggling to control the future, and shrouded, therefore, in a great deal of expressive propaganda. In such cases, it matters more to be convincing than to conform to standards of truth and logic.[21]

A particular cultural group will not necessarily respect the constraints on resource use stemming from the theoretical carrying capacity of land.[22] Rather the knowledge gained from sustainable resource use forms part of the environmental practices of most indigenous populations. It is essential to know what environmental usages are unsustainable, both in the perceptions of the people and in technical terms. Human impacts on the trees are a function not only of numbers of users, but also of the political, economic and social factors that cause individuals to turn to tree products for survival. Sargent and Bass[23] point to the many economic and policy factors outside the forest which marginalize people, forcing them into harvesting trees. Particularly important is a review of policies and practices of land use and land ownership in the agricultural hinterland. It is equally important to look at the factors that attract farmers and loggers into the forest, to encourage them to make the forest productive on a sustainable basis. One of these factors is the high cost of agricultural inputs, particularly fertilizer, seeds and pesticides. If intervention and policy are to be effective in any situation, they must be based on an understanding of these factors.

There is a political aspect in the differential access to natural resources within the local community. Women who want to join the established craft co-operatives are being excluded by the current members. These women stand to lose if the DNR is to carry out its plan of prohibiting unregistered craft-women, should their use of trees be found to be unsustainable.

Another political issue is the position taken by the DNR that the established and registered craft co-operatives, Muusha and Shingirirai, are not damaging the

---

21 K. Milton, *Environmentalism and Cultural Theory: Exploring the Role of Anthropology in Environmental Discourse*, Routledge, London, Milton, 1996, p. 226.
22 M. Redclift, *Sustainable Development: Exploring the Contradictions*, Routledge, London, 1987.
23 S. Sargent and C. Bass, 'The future shape of forests', in Johan Holmberg (ed.), *Policies for a Small Planet*, 2nd edn, Earthscan Publications, 1992.

environment because they are authorized by council. Damage to the environment in this perception is mitigated by whether one pays dues to the council. Such an approach is likely to widen income differentials rather than to alleviate poverty in rural areas and to empower economically even marginalized people. The authorities should note that for many craftworkers, entry into such a venture occurs principally in situations where they are unable to obtain sufficient income from agriculture or wage employment. Therefore policy thrust on utilization of trees to meet rural household needs in Biriwiri should take account of the different roles they play in the strategies of different categories of household.

We have seen that the DNR professionals and some 'outsiders' in Biriwiri hold the view that the women's craft damages the environment and needs to be curbed. This view does not do justice to the people who survive on the craft as a mode of livelihood. For the Biriwiri people, the environment is not about dolphins or whales, toxic waste or the ozone layer, recycled tin cans or newspapers. Instead, it is about resources that contribute directly to family livelihood: water, trees, meadows, wild plants and animals.[24] Environmental aspects of peasant livelihood must be approached, as must other aspects, by discovering the forces acting on individual and social decisions.

In relation to this, Einarsson[25] argues that Icelandic fishermen see campaigns against the hunting of whales as threatening both a way of life and, in the longer run, their right to basic subsistence. In Icelandic fishing villages, there are almost no alternatives to fishing. In Biriwiri the alternative to bark-fibre craft as a mode of livelihood is crop farming, which is beset with difficulties and limitations. Any motivation individuals in Biriwiri might have towards conservation is being eroded by insecurity, instability and stress. These factors make the current struggle for survival more important than securing the future. Such facts of life make people extremely bitter towards those who are seen to be taking away their chances of existence.

---

24 E. Frank, *Peasant Economics: Farm Households and Agrarian Development*, 2nd edn, Cambridge University Press, 1993.
25 N. Einarsson, 'All animals are equal but some are cetaceans: Conservation and culture conflict', in K. Milton (ed.), *Environmentalism: The View from Anthropology*, Routledge, 1993, p. 75.

Chapter 5

Traders and Trees in Nyanyadzi

Stephen Buzuzi and Michael Bourdillon

Department of Sociology, University of Zimbabwe

In any society, resources are defined by what human needs, skill and ability can make of them. Rural people in Zimbabwe often turn to woodland resources to supplement their incomes from farming. Access to such products presents difficulties of control for traditional and civic organizations. Here we examine the ways in which some people utilize tree products, either directly or through trade, creating competing conceptions of conservation.

Human destruction of forests in fragile ecosystems has drawn much attention in development discourse. Environmentalists argue that complete reliance on the primary products of the environment ultimately runs the system down. Consequently, development discourse recommends the implementation of restrictive control and access mechanisms. These strategies have yielded little success. Current policies on the environment lean more to ecological than human needs, which have been held paramount in most of Africa. The models assume neutral positions on the distributional aspects of national policies.

Liberal thinkers explain the environmental crisis in communal areas in terms of property relations and tenure systems, which make sound management impossible. Common policy prescriptions centre on the allocation of full private property rights to individuals. On the other hand, Murombedzi[1] and Campbell[2]

---

1   J. C. Murombedzi, 'Need for appropriate local level common property resource management institutions in communal tenure regimes', Centre for Applied Social Sciences, University of Zimbabwe, Harare, 1990, p. 2.
2   B. Campbell, *et al.*, 'Tree and woodland resources: The technical practices of small-scale farmers', in P. N. Bradley and K. McNamara (eds), 'Living with trees: Policies for forest management in Zimbabwe', World Bank Technical Paper, No. 210, Washington D.C., The World Bank,1993, p. 34.

recognize that every community has internal arrangements to control the use and allocation of natural resource products to its members.

We need to consider human relationships when designing incentives for conservation. Earlier incentives yielded mixed results and have received opposition from their intended beneficiaries. In Muzarabani and Tsholotsho, council has prohibited local people from cutting commercial species, but people disregard the controls and cut the trees for carvings to sell outside their areas.[3] The communities feel that the controls remove their right to nature and interfere with their livelihood.

Economic and socio-structural factors should be considered in the policy process. Restrictive policy forces disadvantaged members of communities further into economic margins unless viable alternatives are available. This study focuses on the positive contributions that the natural environment has in selected household production units. It examines the relationships between ownership of irrigable land, the possession of different assets and implements, social backgrounds and the reliance on woodland resources.

In Zimbabwe, most communities have claims to natural resources through customary use. Interventions by the state and outside agencies displace traditional arrangements, and therefore cannot be easily integrated into the symbolic interpretations of local communities. The dissolution of cultural practices is not likely to result in successful management of resources. Rather, successful policy hinges on understanding the contexts of cultural practices and supporting ongoing local governance systems, through the participation of local communities in the design and implementation of programmes. This is not to suggest that culture is a closed system. Culture is rather a site of heterogeneous borders where different histories, meanings, and experiences intermingle amidst shifting relations of power and privilege.[4]

Godelier[5] pointed out that nature is not external to culture, society or history. Human action and thought transform nature to produce a reality that is simultaneously material and mental. Communities invent different strategies to

---

3   L. Fortmann and C. Nhira, 'Local management of trees and woodland resources in Zimbabwe: A tenurial niche approach', Centre for Applied Social Sciences, University of Zimbabwe, Harare, 1992, p. 10.
4   H. A. Giroux, 'Resisting difference: Cultural studies and the discourse of critical pedagogy', in L. Grossberg et al., Cultural Studies, London and New York, Routledge 1992, p. 205.
5   M. Godelier, The Mental and the Material, Verso, London and New York, 1980, p. 5.

exploit natural resources and to confront the ecological constraints that weigh upon the reproduction of both natural and human resources. These processes imply the development of representations and cultural interpretations of nature, which are shared by members of the community, and the organization of various forms of individual and collective interventions in natural resource conservation. Communities accumulate knowledge of their environments through trial and error. In applying modern knowledge systems, external intervention agencies assume a false dichotomy between nature and its inhabitants. Local communities perceive losses to themselves in the models applied by outside agencies. They adopt defensive strategies to counteract their possible alienation from their environments.

This study explores the relational dynamics between ecological considerations and local perceptions and practices. It shows why some households in Nyanyadzi turn to woodlands for survival. By documenting their circumstances, the study links economics, culture, history, power and inequality.

Methodology

Buzuzi made several visits to the area between March and November 1999, exploring the linkages between household resources and reliance on woodland resources for survival. Household strategies of acquiring a livelihood provided the broad framework for the study. The centre of attention became the incentives for extracting woodland resources. He initially selected a sample of twenty households using woodland resources for a survey of their general background. Five were selected for more detailed study.

He collected data on the circumstances of households through first-hand inquiry, involving individual and group discussions. Views were also taken from a few people not involved in crafts. This combination of sources allowed some measure of the congruence between what the respondents said ought to be done and what they did. Older key informants gave accounts of their experiences in the pre-colonial and post-colonial era.

Historical background

Past national policies affect the general distribution and consumption of resources, and ultimately the quality of rural people's livelihoods. Two historical epochs, the colonial and post-colonial periods, are important in Zimbabwe. The levels of control over the utilization of resources were different, and impacted differently on the environment.

Colonial policy alienated much fertile land and encouraged commercial agriculture conducted by large-scale white farmers. The concentration of black populations in communal areas, and the rapid growth of these populations, put increasing pressure on the natural environment. In places like Nyanyadzi, human settlements encroached upon land unsuitable for cultivation.

The colonial state enacted forest policies to run parallel to the land policies. The Native Forest Produce Act was enacted in 1928. It later became the Natural Resources Act (1942) and the Forest Act (1948). These Acts increased the regulatory powers of the colonial state. Peasant access to forests was restricted to areas that were not commercially profitable. White commercial farming areas exercised voluntary regulation of forests. State interests were in commercial forestry. Africans were not allowed to trade in forest products.

Woodlands cover 53 per cent of Zimbabwe's total land area. About 74 per cent of the country's population live in the communal areas, which constitute 42 per cent of the land and include about 43 per cent of the country's woodlands. Deforestation is more acute in these areas than in the commercial farms and state-protected areas, due to conversion of woodlands into agricultural fields.[6]

Nyanyadzi lies in the Save Valley in Chimanimani District. This area has low rainfall of normally less than 500 millimetres and high temperatures. Due to frequent dry spells, the effective cultivation of most crops is possible only under irrigation. The Nyanyadzi irrigation scheme was established in 1937.

In recent years, immigrants have continued to pour in from surrounding areas. New settlements have opened up the marginal areas around the scheme. These lands are unsuitable for agriculture. Most of the dry-land settlers sell their labour to irrigation landowners, lease land or enter into sharecropping arrangements with elderly irrigation landowners who cannot cultivate all their holdings. Traditional leaders control the allocation of dry land. These settlements are haphazard and some are prone to erosion.

---

[6] Forestry Commission, 'Woodland and tree management programme for dry areas in Zimbabwe', unpublished paper prepared for Overseas Development Agency, 1995, p. 2.

Those who do not lease land resort to extensive agriculture to increase produce from infertile soils. Some farmers have opened up fields along the banks of the Save River. These draw water with cans from the river to water the crops. For some, this has been a viable alternative to owning irrigated land. However, during the 1998-99 season, rainfall in the area was more than normal and crops on the banks of the Save River were swept away.

The land question remains the most enduring legacy of colonialism. VIDCO members reported that new settlements in the margins would not stop. Village head Dirikwe summarizes the problem,

> The size of the irrigation scheme has remained the same. The dam supplying us with water was last re-built in 1964. Since then, we have been lobbying for its expansion to increase its capacity so that we can commission another irrigation scheme. New generations on the land have no fields to plant crops. They are settling anywhere ... We cannot control the settlements. The freedom fighters created a problem for us. The concept of freedom was wrongly defined before independence. Our people were made to believe they can do what they want. Now they do what they want. We have a problem. Chiefs and village heads cannot do anything about it. People say our role died with the end of Rhodesia.

This assertion highlights a new problem of institutions. While the role of pre-independence institutions, as perceived by the Nyanyadzi community, was to harness local resources for centrally planned projects, post-independence institutions – village and ward development committees and rural district councils – set development priorities aimed at revenue generation. The post-colonial state, through the Communal Land Act of 1982, allowed rural district councils to develop land-use plans that override customary land claims. Traditional leaders, however, still hold these customary land claims and retained their role in controlling local patterns of resource use and allocation of land.[7] Competing claims for authority in the control of local resources have emerged. The stewardship of the natural environment remains uncertain as chiefs and village heads have no power to institute sanctions on defaulters. On the other hand, the legally constituted state institutions have neither the legitimacy of customary social structures, nor the resources needed to make them effective.[8]

---

7   J. C. Hatton, 'Status quo assessment of the Chimanimani Transfrontier Conservation Area', a report to Departmento National de Floresta e Fauna Bravia, Maputo, 1995, p. xvi.

8   C. Nhira, *et al.*, 'Communities as institutions for resource management', Centre for Applied Social Sciences, University of Zimbabwe, Harare, 1998, p. 94.

Conflict over knowledge

According to Chikotosa, a marketer of crafts, it is taboo to cut down certain tree species, such as the baobab tree, which is preserved because it is a fruit tree and spirits of the ancestors are believed to reside in the baobab trees. Even when a tree is in a field, one has to go to the chief to seek permission to cut it down. *Mutsha (Xanthocersis zambesiaca)* and *mushuma (Diospyros mespiliformis)* are preserved for their fruit, which provide a source of food during drought periods. *Mutsikiri (Cordia abyssinica)* tree produces a milk-like substance, which is mixed with peanut butter when preparing vegetable relish. *Mukute (Syzygium cordatum)* trees grow along riverbanks, and should not be cut down because they hold water and consequently keep the rivers flowing. Brick moulders, who work on riverbanks close to water sources, have been blamed for cutting down *mukute* trees to burn bricks. *Mukamba (Afzelia quanzensis)* trees have no cultural significance but are preserved for commercial uses. A number of people have been arrested by the police and made to pay fines for cutting down this species.

A stock of indigenous knowledge exists in Nyanyadzi, which, as we saw in the previous chapter, sometimes contradicts official knowledge. Local people prohibit ring barking baobab trees, as this is known to kill them. The Forestry Commission and the Natural Resources Board have prohibited utilizing the bark of the trees on the grounds that it dries out the trees and exposes them to disease. The local people, however, know that the debarked area recovers (*kuundira*) within two years.

To allow longevity and reproduction of the ecosystem, a certain period of time is observed between cutting down mature trees, or in the case of the baobab, when debarking so that it would not be an eyesore to the public. In addition, young growing trees and shoots are not supposed to be cut. In the case of firewood, only dead trees or branches are collected. Living trees are not supposed to be cut down for firewood.

The application of these rules, however, is relative, depending on the purposes for which the wood is to be put. For example, those who require wood for burning bricks, fencing poles or building and roofing materials have to cut down living trees. They seek permission from the chief or village head. He provides a guard to show them the areas and the trees to cut. This is to avoid massive destruction of woodlands through extensive cutting in areas near where the timber is to be used. A tree should be cut at about 50 centimetres off the ground to allow for reshooting. Felling big trees by burning the lower part of the trunks is prohibited. Where mature trees are sparsely populated, one can cut off two branches from a tree with five branches. After cutting a branch, it is a requirement that the person puts soil or paint on the wound to prevent it from exposure to diseases or the heat of the sun.

The Natural Resources Board has advised people not to cut down trees at all. Local people think they can cut down trees without running down the system, and that the existing local rules of harvesting ensure sustainable management of the resources. As a result, the initiatives of the Natural Resources Board have been viewed as coercive conservation. Mai Mujati claimed that without traditional knowledge the whole area would have turned into a desert. Gondo argues that the government claims it has knowledge but that this knowledge does not help the people. The statement is an implied criticism of management programmes initiated by centralized power with little or no local participation. People find it in their interest to support the local rules, which are more flexible.

> *Our chiefs and village heads allow us access to woodland but subject to certain restrictions. How possible is it to deny us access completely. We need firewood, medicines, fibre, construction and craft materials. Our chiefs understand our needs.*

However, there is a difference between what the people say and what they do. Even local rules are sometimes flouted. For example, some people do not seek the chief's permission for cutting trees, because they need more wood than the guards would allow, or because they want to exercise independent discretion with regards to the size, quality and suitability of the tree. Both internal and external controls involve the forfeiture of locals' rights of access to natural resources or the imposition of constraints. Both are viewed as arbitrary closures by some sections of the society, and the environment becomes a political arena. This is because there are multiple realities and shifting interests around the environment, as shaped by the immediate needs of individuals and households. The respondents harvest forest products not only for home use, but also for sale. Most of these people do not have irrigable land. Local authorities have blamed poverty for straining the natural resource base, and flouting rules is attributed to the same problem.

The Chimanimani Rural District Council has issued licences to certain individuals to open craft shops. Holders of licences are not subject to the jurisdiction of local traditional leaders but they are subject to the rural district council, which has the mandate from the state.[9] Holders of licences tend not to be interested in conservation issues. Their licences entitle them even to species subject to sacred controls without social rebuke. Among our respondents, three hold such licences. Most, however, are unwilling to pay $100 for the licences. Buying the licence is equated to giving to government what it does not deserve because trees grow naturally and people should not pay for them.

The locals and the conservationists do not agree on the tree species to be planted in reforestation exercises. Exotic species are popular with management agencies, but the locals perceive little value in them. The exotic eucalyptus has been common on Tree Planting Day. The councillor and the AGRITEX supervisor reiterated that indigenous species should be introduced into the programmes. For example, the *mutsaa* (*Millettia stuhlmannii*) species, which died out in the area in the 1970s, has superior fibre quality to fibre from the baobab, and was traditionally used for door mats, floor mats, dog baskets and bags. The introduction of the *mukamba* species would also be welcome since its wood is used for a variety of craft products – bowls, mortars and pestles, and wooden kitchen utensils.

The case studies

Five cases were studied, comprising two craftsmen, two craft marketers and one person who sourced materials. These cases differed in their resource ownership and the extent of their networks. The first two cases are identical in many fundamental respects: both have developed extensive networks for their products and they produce similar items. The third and fourth cases demonstrate the deprivations within female-headed households and production systems. The fifth case is unique in that the respondent is an unemployed school leaver who has to contribute to the household's livelihood. Lack of skills in crafts compels him to find a role in which skills are not required.

Jonga[10]

Jonga is a middle-aged man, head of a household of seven members. He has five children, two boys and three girls. Three are in primary school and the eldest child in secondary school. His wife is not formally employed, but does house work and plants

---

9   This is only as far as harvesting forest resources is concerned. Traditional leaders do not interfere with licence holders' practices, because the RDC's authority takes precedence over their rule.
10   All names used in this chapter are pseudonyms.

and weeds the fields. Her two daughters assist her with the work. The two boys look after domestic animals – goats, cattle and donkeys – and help in selling craft products when Jonga is away on business.

Jonga has a portion of land in the irrigation scheme. He grows maize in summer and tomatoes, beans and wheat in autumn. He produces these crops both for subsistence and for sale. In a good year he earns about $35,000, well above the minimum wages in agriculture. Jonga owns an ox-drawn plough, a harrow, a scotchcart and two pairs of oxen. He also owns a pick-up truck. He described his possessions as the requisite implements. He hires out his draught power for a fee for ploughing, harrowing, carrying firewood and carting bricks. Between August and October each year, Jonga does not conduct any farming activities. It is a rest period for his family. During this period, he gets his income solely from crafts. He employs hired labour as the need arises.

Jonga started crafts when he lost his job in 1990. He worked as a temporary primary school teacher in Masvingo and he was laid off. The irrigation scheme was facing water shortages then, and there followed the 1992-93 drought, which made many households poorer. Crafts became an option for almost every household. Consequently, the market for craft products was flooded.

The option for Jonga was to extend his market beyond the borders of Nyanyadzi. In these areas, he has established relationships with other craftsmen, marketers and suppliers of materials. These people he called his 'friends'. He can purchase materials on credit. In various places, Jonga has relationships with different craftsmen, who exchange products (materials and finished products) and buy from each other for resale. Jonga explained,

> I specialise in wooden bowls and plates. I am still learning to carve images of wild animals. Those crafts I cannot do, I buy them from others. Those resources I cannot find, I get them from others. They also buy from me. As a result I have a wide range of products for my customers to choose from. Motorists passing through the highway are forced to stop. A well-stocked shop attracts more potential buyers. Buying from others and selling to others in the same trade makes a difference.

Nyanyadzi is Jonga's operating base. He takes the crafts to Beitbridge and has craft shops at Tonhorai near Nyanyadzi, at Maringire along the Masvingo-Beitbridge highway, in Masvingo and Birchenough Bridge. Personal acquaintances and kin in Mutare, Chipinge, Harare, Chimanimani and Chiredzi sell craft products from their homes on his behalf. At each craft-shop, there is a person employed to market the crafts. This

person has accommodation there and receives a monthly salary. Of all his marke
stations, Beitbridge is the most viable. It is strategically located along a busy rout
where he captures tourists and other travellers to and from South Africa.

Jonga established a network through recognizing that his needs and those of h
acquaintances were complementary. He had to negotiate and agree with them o
certain critical issues. The point was not to maximize his gains alone but to reach a
understanding that would optimise their mutual interests. He states that since 199
he has been dealing with the same people and boasts about his use of this resource
He is able to buy a car, feed his family, send his children to school and can emplo
quite a number of people to do his work.

Jonga admits that some tree species are faced with extinction. *Mukamba* species ar
used for making large bowls, doors and plates. These require the use of large log
Large trees are cut down for that purpose. With the increasing number of crafts peopl
huge trees have become scarce save those subject to sacred controls. Jong
acknowledges the benefits to be drawn from conservation programmes – th
preservation of water sources, animal and tree species – but he is also critical of th
activities of the Natural Resources Board and the Forestry Commission. His contentio
is that both bodies have failed to address the problems faced by semi-arid region:
They view crafts as business, and have totally condemned the activity citing the damag
on the environment. Jonga's argument is that in arid regions crafts should be viewe
as another form of subsistence. Agriculture is not reliable due to low rainfall or shortag
of irrigation water.

The Forestry Commission, through liaison with the councillor, local chiefs and headmen
has taken the initiative to plant indigenous species. While he welcomed this initiativ
and pointed to places where trees had been successfully planted, Jonga cited some o
the problems,

> We know we should plant trees. The message has been heard. But the
> authorities do not see the real problem. This is an arid region. It is dry. We
> planted gum trees before. They all wilted because of lack of water.

Jonga cited the lack of incentives as hindering conservation efforts. There are no reward
for individuals who commit their resources and time to conservation. The crisis ir
conservation should not be blamed on individuals in crafts but on authorities, and the
community should come together and find a solution that would address their mutua
interests.

Edzai

Edzai was born in Bulawayo. When he was a child, his parents came to settle in Nyanyadzi, where he grew up. In the mid-1970s he joined the liberation struggle. He came back to Nyanyadzi after the war.

Edzai is married and has two children. He looks after his two younger brothers and a sister to make a household of seven. His wife works in the fields and rears chickens. The brothers help in the fields and the crafts. Edzai is pre-occupied with the crafts, which provide his main income.

He does not have a plot in the irrigation scheme. His dry-land fields are unproductive and very little produce comes from the crops he plants. He has resorted to renting plots from elderly people in the irrigation scheme. He grows beans after the summer maize harvest and stores the produce until November when the product is in short supply. Tomatoes are plenty in June-July and fetch very low prices on the market. Edzai plants the tomato crop in November-December and harvests the crop in March-April when supplies of the crop are short. The produce fetches high prices and the high rentals are absorbed by the high returns.

Edzai owns two ploughs, two scotchcarts and has two pairs of draught oxen. He hires them out at between $120 and $130 per acre. He raises about $4,000 per season from hiring out his oxen.

He joined the woodcraft activity in 1995. Few survival opportunities were open to him given the unreliability of rain-fed agriculture. Crafts were a good alternative because 'we buy only small inputs like glue, polish, sand paper and in some cases wood'. The activity requires little capital to start with. Edzai did not have the money to embark on a project involving an investment.

Edzai sources his own material and does the selling. He employs six boys who assist him. His biggest market is a craft centre at Beitbridge, which buys from him. He also has a consignee near Mutare, who markets the products for a commission. There are women who sell the craft produce in South Africa: they spend two weeks every month in Zimbabwe buying crafts and two weeks in South Africa marketing the craft produce. He claims that he cannot meet the demand for his wooden crafts by the external market.

He encounters a number of constraints in the craft business. Some Natural Resource Committees, who work hand in hand with the chiefs and agents of the Natural Resources Board, monitor the utilization of woodland resources. The Natural Resource Committees show the crafts people the trees to cut down. Trees situated in areas prone to erosion and in sacred places are not supposed to be cut down.

Edzai highlighted that the stocks of trees may be quite good but the quality of the trees for their purposes is deteriorating. That is one of the reasons craftsmen are not co-operating with the agents and the Natural Resource Committees. Once they show the crafts people the trees to cut down, prices are attached to them regardless of the quality of the trees. As a result, craftsmen like Edzai choose to break the rules by not consulting the agents and getting logs for free. These craftsmen opt to pay fines of $500 when they get caught.

In August 1999, Edzai was summoned to a court hearing over the illegal cutting of trees. The police had impounded a truck full of logs travelling from Shinja to Nyanyadzi. According to the summons, Edzai had broken sections of the Chimanimani Rural District Council by-laws. He was given the option of a $500 fine by a Mutare magistrate. The Magistrate made a decision to dispose of the logs by auction. Edzai successfully contracted a woman to bid for them on his behalf.

Edzai vows to continue with the crafts despite the constraints. He contends that government uses the Natural Resources Board to harness local resources and to deprive the local community of these resources. He argues that conservation does not mean prohibition. Rather, the Board and the Forestry Commission should advise the people on methods of harvesting which allow for the regeneration of the forests.

A friend said the land issue was one of the problems facing the nation. He complained that the process is slow and that locals are not given preference on farms acquired by government in areas surrounding Nyanyadzi. Edzai claims that aliens are settled instead. The government has failed to provide viable options and employment for school leavers. Edzai says that what he is doing is enterprising, and does not deserve condemnation.

We are ignored and neglected by our government. The only way to survive is to break the rules. Survival is about taking risks. Some people face starvation because they are risk-averse. We are the inhabitants of this land, and we cannot be stopped from utilizing its resources. We need to survive.

Nobody can stop us from carving crafts. My child does not cry to government for food, but asks for food from the father or the mother. Government is not creating employment. I am unemployed, but I cannot relinquish my fatherly responsibility. I have to feed my family, my dependants. I cannot abdicate that role.

Taku

Taku was born in Nyanyadzi in a polygamous family. Her mother is the first wife and she bore her husband two daughters, Taku being the first. The second wife has five children. Two of them are in primary school, two in secondary school and one is too young to go to school.

Taku dropped out of school after Grade 7 because her mother could not pay school fees after the death of her father, who used to work in a hospital in Chipinge. Taku's sister is mentally unstable and can help only with domestic work. Her mother is elderly and cannot do heavy work. Taku looks after her mother, sister and her two children who are both in primary school. She is not married and she is the household head and the bread-winner.

The proceeds from her father's estate were used in the education of the second wife's children. The household does not have land in the irrigation scheme. Her mother's dry-land field is unproductive. She grows sorghum because it is drought-resistant, and sunflower because it matures early. During good seasons she gets $2,000-$3,000 from agriculture. In recent years, she did not reap anything from the fields because the land is infertile. She has little hope in agriculture and she has shifted her energies to marketing crafts.

Taku augments her income from crafts by selling her labour (*maricho*) in the irrigation scheme. She also sells tomatoes, oranges, mangoes and bananas in Mutare. The greater part of her income comes from crafts, which she buys from local craftsmen and women. Her main wares are wooden plates, bowls, sugar basins, cooking utensils and mats. She pays only deposits for the wares and makes full settlement after sales. This arrangement with the craftspeople makes it possible for her to buy large stocks for resale.

Taku travels long distances to market her products. She takes the wares illegally to Chimoio in Mozambique, where buyers take the products to Beira and to Maputo. She also sells soap, margarine and cooking oil in Mozambique. When returning from Mozambique she buys second hand clothes for sale in Zimbabwe. Barter trading arrangements are common with the Mozambican buyers. Second-hand clothes are easier to sell in Nyanyadzi than the craft products. In some cases, she takes the clothes to Birchenough Bridge or to Mutare.

Taku has tried new markets in the past. In February 1999, she collected $2,000' worth of craft products, which she took to Zambia. She received $6,000 gross. Several times, she has gone to South Africa with wooden bowls, kitchen utensils and fibre mats. The problem with these markets is the high transport costs involved. Moreover, her mother and sister need her care. She cannot go to town to look for formal employment, because with her education she could not acquire a well-paying job. She resolved, however, to develop her networks in crafts further and improve her financial management skills. At the time of this study, Taku attended a workshop on small business development held at Chimanimani Hotel in November 1999.

Kumwe

Kumwe is a divorcee in her 50s. She has three children, all grown up, and working in Harare. After she was divorced she came back to stay with her parents in the mid-1980s, who have 1.25 acres in the irrigation scheme. Kumwe has no land of her own, but helps her elderly parents. Her parents are pay for farming inputs like seeds, draught power, fertilisers, and sometimes labour to plant and weed. She explains,

> I do most of the work but that does not entitle me to the proceeds. I have no land and after all I am not supposed to be staying with parents. I had my own home where I was married. It is out of their goodwill that I am here. I have brothers who have a right of inheritance. If I say the land is mine, I would destabilise the family. I can only do that out of greed.

Kumwe supervises hired labour. She does most of the weeding and watering of plants. She grows vegetables for sale. She took $2,000 from beans in 1999. Maize is produced mainly for subsistence. She cannot sell the maize because she has to keep enough to ensure against future crop failures due to prolonged dry spells and water shortages. Her brothers and children in town also take grain from the family granary because food is expensive in town. But there are few remittances from them even if they work.

Kumwe draws grain for daily consumption from the same granary. She is satisfied with the household production and consumption arrangements. However, she stressed her need to earn income to buy her necessities. She makes fibre doormats, hats, bags and dog baskets. Those wares that she cannot make herself, like wooden cooking utensils, sugar basins, plates and floor mats, she buys from travelling traders (*vafambi*). Her parents assist her by purchasing raw materials if the traders pass through when Kumwe is not at home, and she pays them back from the profits. She buys most of the wooden items from traders from Bangwe and Changazi village near Nyanyadzi.

Kumwe sells small wares that are cheap and bring in small profits. She does not have much money to buy the more expensive products. She does not want to take the risk of keeping large sums of money in stocks before they are bought. Expensive wares rarely have quick returns unless they are unique in the market. She has not taken her market beyond the borders of Nyanyadzi, largely because her wares are too common. She fears she would board buses to certain places to come back without sales. Also, her parents need her care at home. Her weekly sales range from twenty to $600. She rarely gets more than $200. She would have opted to sell her labour *(maricho)* but that strains her considering her age and the fact that she does most of the work at home.

Vhukile

Vhukile completed 'O' levels in 1996 and passed three subjects. After his 'O' levels he went to Chipinge, where he stayed with a cousin, to look for employment. He returned to Nyanyadzi in late 1997 after failing to secure employment. For a short period in 1998, Vhukile was employed by a local builder. This man passed away shortly after taking Vhukile on.

Originally, the family lived in Buhera. They migrated to Nyanyadzi in the mid-1980s because there was sickness in the family and a neighbour was believed to be bewitching them. Vhukile's father works at a farm in Nyazura. His mother sells vegetables at Birchenough Bridge. He stressed that the family faces acute food shortages throughout the year. Remittances from the father are minimal because he earns very little. Vhukile's mother has to toil to make sure that the family has enough to eat. Their homestead and fields are situated on barren soil out of the irrigation scheme. The food shortages are largely due to the unproductive soil, coupled with unreliable rainfall.

There are nine in the household. Vhukile has three brothers and three sisters, four of them in secondary school, where the fees are a problem for his parents. Sometimes the children are sent away from school for failing to pay fees. The household is sometimes saved by the demand for its labour in the irrigation scheme. Annually the household raises around $3,000 from weeding. The money usually goes towards the payment of school fees and the purchase of school uniforms.

None in the family has the skills, or the tools, to make things like doormats, floor mats, baskets or wooden crafts. Consequently, Vhukile sources materials for other people, a task that requires energy rather than skill. His main work is stripping baobab bark. His sisters and brothers assist by carrying the fibre home and selling it to people who make bags, doormats and floor mats. He uses a specific measure called *mbomba* and charges $25. There is always a ready market for the fibre but it sometimes requires walking long distances searching for customers. The task of stripping requires much energy. Most women find it arduous and opt to buy the fibre. Some craftspeople in the irrigation scheme do not have time to strip fibre because they have to work in their fields.

Vhukile also sources materials for craftsmen who carve wooden bowls, plates and images of wild animals. These require logs from big trees. The rules are often broken. Vhukile admits that he sometimes goes to the woodlands at dusk to cut down big trees when he has orders from the craftsmen. Sometimes it takes two days to complete the task of cutting the logs into smaller pieces and hiding them in safe places. At dusk or dawn, his sisters and brothers carry the logs home or to the craftsmen's workshops. Vhukile reported that once, in July 1999, the village head's guards waited in hiding at a place where he had felled a tree to see who had done it. He did not go to that place after being tipped off by one of his customers. Vhukile admits he has contributed to the environmental crisis through these activities but has somehow been exonerated.

Vhukile pointed out that there are many ways of evading rules. Craftsmen require different sizes of logs. The rule laid down by local headmen is that those who carve smaller items like walking sticks and cooking utensils can utilize residues left by those who carve mortars, large bowls and images of wild animals. Those who collect residues, 'scavengers', can do so openly during the day. In practice, the scavengers cut down the trees at odd hours and carry the logs for sale to craftsmen of large bowls. When they collect the residues during the day, they appear to observe the rules.

Some shop owners, teachers and retired people buy firewood from Vhukile. It is big business in winter. He stocks firewood at home even when he does not have orders. Shop owners and teachers pay well for the service.

Vhukile highlighted that the Natural Resources Board interventions are not effective because people need to meet their practical needs. Few options are available to them so they turn to woodlands for survival.

Comments of a VIDCO member

Nhau has participated in a VIDCO since 1980 and his experience and knowledge of the problems of conservation in Nyanyadzi provide important insights into the crisis, particularly with respect to relations between local institutions and the community. The existence of explicit rules about how woodland resources should be harvested has not saved the forests.

First, Nhau calls for a critical look at the people whose survival and livelihoods depend on woodlands. These households display some signs of deprivation. Prohibitionist conditions adversely affect their livelihoods. Crafts have become their most feasible option for survival. Nhau reiterated that the people have learned to move from rules to strategies and to manipulate the rule of customary law. They work against the rules because of poverty. Many households outside the irrigation scheme survive through harvesting forest products. Attempts at social control have created a conflict between aesthetic and practical needs, the former being the value system for the rich and the latter for the poor.

The councillor encourages tree planting and has a nursery from which people can collect gum trees and others for planting. Nhau was one of the several people who utilized this facility. But many members (about half those interviewed) of village and ward development committees lacked knowledge or awareness of these issues. Indeed, some members appeared to have little interest in any of the functions of their committees, arguing that they received no remuneration for committee work.

This lack of awareness cannot be fully blamed on the committees. Some blame must also fall on the government officials who are supposed to educate the leaders and to disseminate information to the grassroots. AGRITEX, for example, does not extend its services beyond the irrigation scheme. Chiefs and village heads allocate land in the dry lands without conducting land surveys. Marginal lands have been turned into cultivated areas. Consequently, the conversion of forests into fields has increased in recent years.

There is generally a low level of environmental awareness within the community. Nhau stressed that the people think that trees grow naturally and that no one should claim the stewardship of what grows naturally. Consequently, people define their right to nature in unlimited terms. This presents problems of control of resource utilization. The Forestry Commission's target group for their message on annual tree planting days has been wrong. They have focused on schools. Campaigns have not reached households, and if they have, it has been only once a year. Little time and effort has been given to educate the adults on the importance of sustainable environmental management. The authorities respond only to immediate crises, for example, a threatening gully, then they go away.

People do what they want, as their needs dictate, and turn a blind eye to the rule of law because local authorities have no power to impose sanctions. The police have such powers and they are a real restraint to unapproved behaviour in the community.

Chiefs and village heads have influence in the community but they are not aware of a mandate from the state to be overseers of the resources. Although they are traditionally the custodians of the land and its resources, their powers have been handed over to rural district councils. The result has been competition over the control of the resources. Rural district councils are supposed to monitor the sale of the resources. Chiefs allegedly receive bribes and allow their people to harvest without the council's knowledge. Some village heads support baobab strippers despite the Natural Resources Board prohibitions, saying their people are poor and they survive on this activity.

There is thus a noticeable lack of co-operation from all sections of society. Nhau argues that it is not possible for anyone to cut down trees and carry the logs by vehicle or scotchcart without someone witnessing it. Those witnesses do not come forward to report offenders. Local traditional leaders refuse the responsibility of dealing with offenders, saying that this is the task of the police, the Natural Resources Board, the Forestry Commission or the rural district council. This lack of co-operation is induced by fears of witchcraft. Even if the authorities are given the power to impose sanctions on offenders, those powers are not effective. The authorities argue that witchcraft is difficult to prove and they would not find redress in the case of being harmed because the Witchcraft Suppression Act protects witches. They cannot conduct witch-hunts or accuse their adversaries of witchcraft. Nhau stressed that many households deal in witchcraft, with some being well-known for harming others. These households are difficult to control and they do what they want.

Household livelihoods and woodlands

Production both in agriculture and in craft products has remained a necessary condition to sustain a constant flow of income into households for survival. Holders of dry lands obtained significant incomes from the woodlands, through selling crafts and firewood, burning bricks or repairing fences for a fee. For these households, agriculture is not a viable alternative, and increased income from craft production has a marked impact on standards of living, acquisition of assets, nutritional status, consumption patterns, savings and school fees for children and clothing. Several members of a single family are likely to participate in the extraction of forest resources. The recognition in the household that increased craft production is a viable option speeds the transfer of skills from producers to other family members. Skills pass from parents to offspring at very young ages. Children have strong career influences within the households and subsequently add on to the number of producers in the family. In the households studied, small boys participate in simple woodcrafts like carving walking sticks or kitchen utensils. Girls of primary school age make bags and door mats.

The irrigators, on the other hand, obtain most of their incomes from agriculture and reported that they spent little time on craft production. Nevertheless, their livelihoods can be uncertain. Uncertainties can partially be resolved by recourse to forest products. Between planting and marketing, irrigators have to wait for a prolonged periods without receiving any income. Certain buyers of agricultural produce buy on credit and delays in payment were cited as one of the reasons leading irrigators to exploit forest resources. Moreover, the sizes of plots have remained the same over the years despite the increase in the size of families. Some irrigators reported that they did not sell any agricultural produce because their produce is not even sufficient for the subsistence needs of the household.

Discussion

Authorities in Nyanyadzi attribute the problem of woodland degradation to business motives by local people. In a bid to reduce trade in woodland products, the Chimanimani Rural District Council has promulgated various by-laws, and chiefs and headmen have imposed social sanctions. The aggressive approach of authorities has led to what can be called 'cultural parallelism', in which two conservation cultures are locked in competing and contradictory outlooks, each defending its own identity.[11] Since culture is central to the conflicts, it must play a leading part in resolving the conflicts and in future sustainable management.

This study shows that the factors influencing the trends in environmental degradation are more social and complex. Communities tolerate change that does not threaten their personal identity, values and beliefs, skills and capabilities, behaviour and personal environment. The inhabitants of the environment seek to maximize the resourcefulness of their culture and their environment.

Lower income groups dominate the use of woodland resources. Stopping the extraction of forest resources without addressing the inherent socio-structural inequalities will not only push some households into extreme poverty but will also

---

11   E. Thomas and M. Woods, *The Manager's Casebook*, Duncan Peterson, London, 1992, p. 217.

be met with formidable resistance from members of the community. There are too many incentives and justifications for exploiting the woodlands. Proceeds from forest products have played a fundamental role in raising the standards of living of many households. Some individuals have expanded their activities to a level of accumulation and trade, and have little else on which to practise their entrepreneurial skills.

The penetration of the state into rural peripheries has affected the distribution and consumption of natural resources.[12] This is coupled with parallel authority structures: multi-stranded claims to authority have resulted in competing claims for the control of local resource use in most communal areas in Zimbabwe. Local culture interprets political institutions as instruments of cultural oppression, designed by government deny the capacities of the people. The demand for devolution of authority to the grassroots is a legacy of social inequality, cultural difference and political struggles over the years.

State intervention may be justified where national wealth, equity and the need for ordered policy implementation are concerned. However, the state has been dismissed in Nyanyadzi as an agent of conservation because centralized programmes are associated with the forfeiture of the rights of locals to access to their natural environment. The Natural Resources Board prohibits people from cutting down trees, thereby depriving people of firewood, medicines, fibres and construction materials among others. The rural district council issues licences to some individuals to open craft shops. Those without licences said the licences were a sign of how government promotes inequality within societies. While traditional chiefs and headmen, by virtue of their flexible regulations, are perceived as promoting the material interests of their society, state institutions are characterized as not representing the interests of the community.

Apart from paying insufficient attention to the needs of local communities, current interventions have ignored existing knowledge structures and value systems. While chiefs allow their people access to woodlands subject to internal controls, the Natural Resources Board has maintained a prohibitive position. The chiefs' flexible approach allows the community to meet its needs, and receives its support. Ideally, this traditional system of authority should have been utilized more fully.

---

[12] See A. P. Cheater, 'Anthropologists and policy in Zimbabwe: Design at the centre, and reactions on the periphery', in R. Grillo and A. Rew (eds), *Social Anthropology and Development Policy*, Tavistock Publications, London and New York, 1985, p. 68.

The Natural Resources Board and the community do not agree on conservation methods. This is evident in contrary views on the effects of reaping bark from baobab trees. For successful management of culture change, methods that complement existing knowledge may prove effective.

The respondents all agree on the need for proper environmental management, but their social and economic circumstances of poverty compel them to defy regulations. The restriction of access to tree resources is likened to a deprivation of livelihood, especially for those in the dry areas. In their eyes, such restrictions are to do with aesthetics rather than ethics. They defend their practice by reference to their historical rights to resources.

Chapter 6

'We Came to the Bridge for Money': Prostitution at a Rural Service Centre

Ishmael Magaisa

Department of Sociology, University of Zimbabwe

The history of prostitution in Zimbabwe, and in other countries in sub-Saharan Africa, is closely associated with urbanization and other processes of capitalist development in towns, mines and farming settlements. This link between sex work and 'foreign' aspects of socio-economic life created the myth that sex work was predominantly an urban phenomenon. Rural areas were seen as uncontaminated bastions of culture, free from the 'evils' of urban life. Not surprisingly, many studies of prostitution were conducted in urban areas with little regard to the rural dimensions of sex work. This chapter shifts the focus and context of prostitution to rural Zimbabwe and explores its causes, dynamics, organization and perceived costs and benefits by rural actors at Birchenough Bridge rural service centre. I argue that sex work in rural Zimbabwe is a form of livelihood that mirrors the social expectations placed on women as well as the cultural organization of gender relations.

Whilst male promiscuity is tolerated in Zimbabwe, female prostitution or sex work remains a seriously contested form of sexuality. Prostitution is not illegal, but loitering and soliciting are. Women suspected of prostitution are often arrested and made to pay fines. Moral crusaders have for some time advanced moral, religious and cultural arguments to urge society to act against prostitution. However, sex work has not declined but is on the increase. Prostitution has now spread to rural areas and involves children as young as nine years old.

It is against this background that I set out to investigate sex work at Birchenough Bridge between 1998 and 1999 using observation, interviews and group discussions. Birchenough Bridge is located in south-eastern Zimbabwe, along the main road that connects the towns of Mutare, Masvingo, Chipinge and Chiredzi. There is no industry at Birchenough Bridge, and the service centre lies in a very low-yielding agricultural region that relies heavily on irrigated crops for subsistence. A significant part of town's population consists of petty commodity traders, travellers, tourists and vendors of various kinds. These are occupations that involve school children.[1] The mobile population of the centre created conditions that are generally conducive to prostitution.[2]

Many people at Birchenough Bridge are travellers and had no accommodation of their own. Poor travellers and vendors slept on shop verandas while those with money either booked hotel rooms or hired prostitutes from whom they got both accommodation and sexual services. Because hotel rooms were more expensive than sexual fees, many travelling males preferred to hire prostitutes than to pay hotel bills. One of my female respondents said, *'Vanouya kwatiri nokuti isu tinovabata zvakanaka nokuvapa pamberi nopokuvata'* (They come to us because we handle them well by providing sexual pleasure as well as decent accommodation).

My key informant, Nyarai, who worked at the local hotel as a waitress, told me that there were about 50 prostitutes in the town. My own counting put the figure at between 30 and 40. During group discussions, however, the figure of 200 emerged. Participants in these discussions argued that a significant number of prostitutes operated secretly. These 'hidden' sex workers consisted of female traders who engaged in part-time prostitution and schoolgirls who were desperate to hide their prostitute identities in this small community, in case they were ridiculed, beaten and called names.

Nevertheless, I was surprised to find that rural women did not resist being researched, unlike female sex workers in urban Harare, whom I had studied previously. Although rural women had suffered harassment by the police and been made to pay fines like their urban counterparts, fear of the police and local traditional leaders was not a priority on their list of concerns. Rural sex workers

---

[1]   M. F. C. Bourdillon and M. Mutisi, 'Child vendors at a rural growth point', in M. F. C. Bourdillon (ed.), *Earning a Life: Working Children in Zimbabwe*, Harare, Weaver Press, 2000.

[2]   Studies in the history of sexuality have established a link between mobile populations and prostitution. See R. Littlehood, *Anthropology Today*, Vol. 13, No. 2, 1997, pp. 1-16, and J. Vickers, *Women and War*, Zed Books, London, 1993.

were on the whole co-operative, frank and seemed not to bother about the stigma of being labelled 'whores'. Perhaps this was because for them, prostitution was more a matter of survival than a question of morality. I found it interesting that the women were not ashamed of their job and openly declared, *'Pabrigde takavinga mari'* (We have come to the Bridge for money).

The moral dimensions of rural research however continued to feature throughout the interviews and group discussions. The women wanted to know what I was going to do about their situation and what solutions I had to the problem of prostitution. I found these questions difficult to answer. As I struggled to explain to them that academic researchers merely want to know what is happening and make recommendations to policy makers, I could see signs of disapproval as the women wondered why I was wasting their time investigating a problem for which I had no solutions. One respondent then asked, *'Ko imi hamugoni here kutitsvakira madonor anogona kutibatsira pakurarama kwedu'* (But can't you find us donors who can assist us?) After assuring them that I was going to do something about it, the women thanked me in advance and castigated researchers who do nothing to assist the researched. One women said,

> Vamwe vanhu vanongouya vachiti makondomu, makondomu vanofunga kuti tinodya makondomu here isu *(Some researchers come here saying condoms, condoms, do they think that we feed on condoms?)*

The concerns of these women raise a variety of ethical issues related to academic research. First, should researchers merely extract information from respondents in difficult circumstances and leave without offering something in return? Second, what packages must the researcher bring to the researched? Third, do academics have enough financial and material resources to change the world they study? It appears to me that answers to these questions have serious implications for the sustainability of research projects and the securing of co-operation from respondents.

The participant group and their demographic characteristics

The participant group consisted of nine women whose ages ranged between fifteen and 32 years. Seven of the women had one or two children who they had either left with their mothers in rural homes, or kept with them. I chose to focus mainly on women who conducted their business from shacks or rented accommodation at Birchenough Bridge because of their relative permanence in the town. Two or three women and their children shared the rooms. A significant number booked hotel rooms at Birchenough Bridge Hotel. However, they did not pay daily rates a was required of other visitors. While the normal fee for overnight stay at the local hotel was $350, the women only paid a rental fee of $150 per month. These preferential rates were either intended to attract clients or because it made more economic sense to rent to the women rooms that would otherwise be unoccupied

The women came from surrounding rural districts and growth points such a Bikita, Masvingo, Chipinge, Chibuwe, Nyika, Buhera, Chisumbanje, Zaka and some catchment area communities. They said they engaged in prostitution because they were unmarried (which denied them male breadwinners), poor and lacked skills. The decision to operate at Birchenough Bridge was determined by both the productivity of sex labour and the convenience of operating near home. Operating nearer home ensured the women maximum social security such as increased contac with kin, regular and accurate information about family members, cheap food and investment of profits. In times of trouble, they could relocate home quickl and cheaply. Muzvidziwa[3] found similar social and economic considerations among single women in Masvingo. However, working nearer home had disadvantages in that it could reduce returns if potential clients included a section of her kin with whom it was taboo to have sex. Also, merely being known to be a prostitute in conservative rural Zimbabwe can undermine a woman's chances of marriage.

Seven clients were observed and interviewed. They refused to take part in group discussions, saying that they did not want to be known as people who purchased sex. Part of clients' refusal to discuss prostitution as a group can be explained by the fact that whereas sex workers were relatively homogeneous, clients were very heterogeneous in terms of composition. One reason for purchasing sex included the desire for sexual variety: '*Toda kunzwa kuti dzepano pa Birchenough Bridge dzinonaka sei.*' (We want to find out how good the women are here at Birchenough Bridge.) Male traders, bus drivers and their crews claimed to have stayed too long in the bush (*Tagarisa tiri musango*), saying they wanted to relieve sexual pressure. Others claimed addiction to sex: '*Handigoni kurara ndega* (I cannot sleep alone).

---

3   V. Muzvidziwa, 'Rural-urban linkages: Masvingo's double-rooted female heads of household' *Zambezia*, Vol. 24, No. 2, 1997.

Although kinship considerations were important in influencing the women's decision to operate nearer home, the social relationships of prostitutes were affected by rural discourses on prostitution. In response to public criticism and condemnation of their profession, the women developed strategies that enabled them to protect their own interests, manage their identities and accommodate a variety of demands placed upon them by other social actors such as community leaders, parents, clients and other prostitutes.

The rural discourse on prostitution in Zimbabwe and its impact on prostitutes' social relationships

Sexuality in rural Zimbabwe resembles traditional sexual norms and values. Although some sexual expectations are changing due to European influence and popular culture, traditional sexual morality demands that all adult women be married to one man, bear him children, work in the fields and be good wives and not witches. The single female invites social ridicule, punishment, disparaging labels and even violence. This is the case for single mothers, whether they are widowed, divorced or single by choice, and for prostitutes and homosexuals. Single mothers at Birchenough Bridge, for example, were referred to as *mvana* or *zvarakamwe* – derogatory terms used to indicate the moral bankruptcy of unmarried women who have children. While there is concerted effort to censure female sexuality, men are allowed sexual variety through polygamy, and promiscuity is part of the culture of masculinity in Zimbabwe.

It is against this background of traditional sexual double standards that the practice of prostitution in Zimbabwe's rural areas must have come as a surprise, and even a shock, to many rural people. Many traditional leaders like chiefs, headmen and spirit mediums felt scandalised by prostitution. They said it was immoral and likely to offend ancestral spirits with disastrous consequences for local communities. In rural Zimbabwe, natural disasters such as drought and failure of crops, and calamities such as AIDS, are often given a spiritual explanation and blamed on prostitutes and other 'deviant' people whose behaviour is perceived as disrespectful to local cultures. It is in this context that a local *sabhuku* (headman) at Birchenough Bridge once spearheaded a crusade to rid the town of prostitutes. He argued that sex workers operating at the service centre were from 'foreign' lands and that they were likely to contaminate the morals of local women. He further argued that prostitution was contributing to a culture of laziness and consequent low agricultural production as most participants in sex work either succumbed to AIDS or spent most of their time hanging around bars and drinking. Despite such attempts to remove prostitutes from the area, prostitution continued to exist partly because of large-scale poverty and, as already argued, because Birchenough Bridge service centre provides a market for sexual commodities.

The women resisted eviction arguing that if the headman and other self-appointed rural custodians of culture were totally against prostitution, then they had to provide them with food and clothes. They accused local leaders of contributing to their predicament by failing to assist them when they were in need.

The women pointed to a number of factors that had forced them into prostitution. The prostitutes said that their husbands had neglected them, denied fathering their children, divorced them or refused to pay them maintenance. The women blamed boyfriends whose interests in women were only sexual, leaders who condemned prostitutes yet utilized their services and relatives who told them what is good or bad without providing practical solutions to their economic problems. At the time of research there was much discussion about drafting a new constitution for Zimbabwe. When asked what they wanted in this constitution, the women suggested that the law should make it very difficult for men to deny paternity. They said that men ought to be legally obliged to pay maintenance, and they said that it should be made illegal for men to divorce women with whom they have had children. In a sense, sex workers at Birchenough Bridge were lamenting the ineffectiveness of the modern extended family, and a weak social security system that fails to assist vulnerable members of society and the double standards of a dual morality.

The prostitutes further argued that there was no link between prostitution and drought. They said that these were excuses constructed by spirit mediums and other rural holders of cultural capital to justify the victimization of sex workers. Prostitutes recognized that droughts were caused by natural climatic conditions rather than by the anger of local rainmakers. The women pointed out that they did not own land and plots in the irrigation schemes nearby, and the community could not expect them to starve just because of abstract conformity to morality. They complained that even if they wanted to get married, few man were prepared to marry 'mvana'. Even if they were lucky enough to be married, men did not want to look after their children from previous marriages. Yet there is a Shona saying which states, 'Adhonza sanzu andhonza nemashizha aro' (He who pulls the branch of a tree pulls it together with its leaves), which means that men who marry single mothers must look after their children as well.

Societal attitudes towards sex work have important implications for the way prostitutes viewed themselves, and the ways in which they were perceived by non-prostitute members of society. These perceptions in turn affected social interaction. Some prostitutes said that their parents and relatives had rejected them. This was particularly the case with schoolgirls who had played truant from school and fallen pregnant during their sexual adventures with men. Prostitutes whose parents had expected bridewealth from the marriage of their daughters reported hostile relationships: the parents confirmed their hostility. Stella, the only daughter in a family of six, reported that her mother was bitter that she had become a prostitute, and refused to see her as long as she remained a prostitute. Other prostitutes reported that their relatives did not want to associate with them for fear that they or their children would be influenced by them and also become prostitutes. Although this public perception of prostitutes as morally contagious reflected legitimate concerns in so far as prostitutes were responsible for the recruitment and occupational socialization of new recruits, it failed to distinguish prostitution from what prostitutes do and think. Ninety per cent of my respondents did not want their children or relatives to become prostitutes. To illustrate this point, one prostitute tried to beat her fifteen-year-old daughter who had become a prostitute. The daughter ran away and was sharing a room with a friend who was also a prostitute.

Although it was difficult to disguise prostitution at a small rural growth point such as Birchenough Bridge, my respondents devised techniques of identity management that were intended to achieve social acceptability in a community that was generally hostile to sex workers. The women told their mothers and sisters that they were prostitutes, but lied to their fathers and brothers, telling them that they were either domestic workers or petty commodity traders. The task of disguising prostitution was easier among women who combined prostitution with vending. This enabled them to lie about their sources of income. However, successful lying depended on there being sufficient geographical distance between the parents' residential area and the daughter's work place. Prostitutes also discouraged family members from visiting them at their work place in case they guessed at their survival strategies.

A major requirement affecting the social relations of both rural and urban black people of Zimbabwe is financial assistance to parents and relatives. Prostitute daughters who contributed significantly to the upkeep of their kin by providing material and financial support were able to negotiate social acceptability to the extent that there were major links between prostitutes and their mothers, aunts and sisters. The few resources that prostitutes had were invested in the maintenance of these vital links.

The material and financial contributions by prostitutes could be seen in the context of negotiating and buying influence and recognition in family and community power structures.[4] A community is a constellation of power relations: when a daughter contributes to the family, she purchases space within the family and is therefore able to enjoy some freedom. Many parents of prostitutes reported that they were getting significant assistance from their daughters. One old man was very thankful to his prostitute daughter for paying his hospital bill and for sending a brother to school. If daughters are more useful to their parents than sons then there is conflict between ideology and practice in so far as patriarchy prefers male children.

The organization and marketing of sex at Birchenough Bridge

The women were hired in two major ways: 'short-time' sex, which was measured by a single ejaculation, and 'take-away' sex, which involved the client having sexual access to a woman for the whole of a night. Clients paid between twenty and $50 for 'short-time' sex and between $100 and $150 for 'take-away' sex. Respondents told me that these fluctuations in prices were determined by market demand, the social status of the client and how desperate a particular prostitute was for money. If the client was a mere vendor, prostitutes tended to charge less. If the client was a teacher, they charged more. Regular clients were charged less because they contributed to the well-being of the women in other ways. Client bus drivers were known to offer free transport to their prostitute girlfriends.

The women claimed that they made about $1,000 every month. Much of the money was reinvested into prostitution by buying attractive clothes in order to

---

4   See C. Oppong's argument that married women in Accra who have resources are able to exercise more independence within their families, C. Oppong, 'Middle class African marriage – A family study of Ghanaian civil servants', Allen Unwin, London, 1981, pp. 112-122.

remain competitive. According to one respondent, '*Varume havadi vakadzi vane tsvina*' (Men do not want dirty women). In order to compete effectively, the women had to be smart and presentable.

The clients were divided into three categories: local regular clients, who were referred to as *mapermanent* (permanent clients), local non-regular clients, and non-locals. In the category of local clients were teachers, vendors and employees of the Zimbabwe Electricity Supply Authority and the Department of Agricultural Extension Services (the two main employers of permanent staff in the town). Clients in the non-local category included bus drivers and their crews, truck drivers and travellers of various kinds passing through Birchenough Bridge. Men who missed buses hired prostitutes in order to secure accommodation. However, non-local clients who spent nights at a prostitute's shack risked confrontation with the woman's regular boyfriend. To avoid conflict with permanent clients, some non-local clients with money hired prostitutes and took them to hotel rooms for the night.

The permanent clients were very possessive and claimed a monopoly over their prostitute 'wives'. As in monogamous marriages, the women were denied the right to take in other clients and were always expected to be available when the permanent wanted them. These demands curtailed the income-generating capacities of the women. For example, if a prostitute was hired by a client with more money than her regular boyfriend, the latter would demand compensation (*mari yandakambokupa kare*). Although permanent clients sometimes looked after the welfare of these women, they refused to pay for sex arguing that '*iwe une ESAP yako*' (you have your own structural adjustment programme and I have my own). The women complained that even though permanent clients gave them about $500 every month, the amount was very little compared to what they got as freelance prostitutes.

Such ambiguous prostitute-client relationships, which mirrored characteristics of traditional love and marriage, curtailed the women's freedom and contributed to gender conflict. I asked the women during group discussions why they had these permanent clients if they were an economic liability? The women told me that permanent clients guaranteed them a constant supply of both sex and material resources during hard times when they had no clients, and when the women were arrested by the police, the permanent clients paid fines.

It was not only permanent clients who demonstrated a desire to control, own and use prostitutes to their own advantage. Non-permanent clients also sometimes refused to pay for the sexual services rendered arguing, '*Tose tanakirwa saka mubhadharo wacho ndewey*' (We both enjoyed so why should I pay you?). In other instances the client would pay only to demand the money back, accusing the women of not having performed satisfactorily. The women referred to this client practice as *demando*. In other cases, clients would pay only to steal the money later. The more unfortunate women were assaulted for turning down proposals of certain men. Such men would ask the women why they had come to the bar if they did not want to be hired ('*Saka wavingeyi kubhawa kana uchindiramba'*). Men assumed that women went to bars specifically to be hired, a factor that has contributed to the harassment of many non-prostitute women who decide to relax in both rural and urban bars.

Although the women lived in constant fear of sexual violence, they perceived the various forms of violence they encountered as occupational hazards. They had also devised methods of dealing with 'criminal' clients. There have been cases of women, either individually or in groups, who have physically beaten men who refused to pay for services or in other ways abused the women. Another technique is to confiscate the property of clients who refused to pay or to deny sexual services to such clients.

There is some competition among prostitutes in the search for clients, and conflict can arise over certain aspects of sex work such as '*kutorerana maclients*' (taking each other's clients), resulting in threats of violence from other women. Nevertheless, the women also practised gender solidarity in dealing with troublesome clients. They also show solidarity in socializing new members and lending each other money.

Confronting health issues: A rural sex worker perspective

Table 1 below shows STD statistics of Buhera district where Birchenough Bridge lies from 1991 to 1999.

Table 1: STD statistics for Buhera and Birchenough Bridge

Year	Buhera District	Birchenough Bridge
1991	9,483	2,625
1992	10,310	2,765
1993	7,094	2,482
1994	11,715	2,100
1995	8,557	2,249
1996	8,135	2,005
1997	7,381	1,318
1998	8,480	1,871
1999	7,748	1,035
Total	78,903	18,450

Source: Buhera District Hospital 1999

There are no adequate figures for the population of Birchenough Bridge, but it is assumed to be around 10,000. In this case, the figures show an average of one case per year per every five of the population. The decrease in recent years may be due to a decrease in cases or simply to a decrease in hospital attendance. The population of Buhera according to the 1992 census was 203,739.

All my respondents thought that prostitution was a problem not in the moral sense but because their chances of contracting diseases were very high. One of my respondents summarized the problem as follows:

> *Every day you have sex with a different man and at times you have sex with more than one man per day. In most cases you sleep with someone whom you hate, despise or do not love. Moreover you can be forced to have sex with those people who refuse to use condoms. During sex you are not expected to refuse because he has paid his money. It's a big problem, zvinouraya (it kills).*

She is lamenting the absence of choice. However, this should not be understood as prostitutes' failure or refusal to make decisions in matters pertaining to their health. The context of prostitution itself is structurally inhibitive. The women were aware of AIDS and had seen a lot of their friends in this profession dying, but they argued that *'hapana basa risingaurayi'* (there is no job that does not kill). It is true that all jobs somehow kill but some kill more than others do. In particular, the way prostitution is practised in both urban and rural Zimbabwe increases the risks of infection.

The women knew the various ways of preventing AIDS infection and they carried condoms, which they collected from the local health centre. Because it is now fashionable to be known to use condoms, my respondents claimed to use them but the reality is that they did not use them during sex. This emerged during group discussions where the women complained of repeated sexually transmitted diseases. Accusations of infecting each other with STDs (*wakandirumisa*) were common and medical statistics at Birchenough hospital testified to the non-use of condoms as many patients were treated for STD infections.

Generally the decision to use condoms rested with clients, a factor which reduced the women's control over the sexual encounters. While seven of the nine male clients interviewed claimed to use condoms, the other two, who knew that they were already infected with HIV, did not. In the words of one female respondent, '*Vanongoda kupushira vamwe*' (They just want to push the disease onto others). Some clients even went to the extent of urinating (not ejaculating) inside the women. It is such clients who were a health problem particularly if the women were desperate for money because then they would not insist on the use of condoms. Not surprisingly, some poor prostitutes argued that it was better to die of AIDS than to die of hunger: '*Hapana kusiri kurwara chero nzara inorwadza*'.

The women also took measures to minimize infection. Such measures included putting foam rubber or cotton wool or tissues inside their vaginas before sex to absorb fluids, taking a shower soon after sex and certain traditional medicines. I asked them why they did not use female condoms and they replied that both male and female condoms resulted in itching after sex. Some traditional medicines were also known to cause pain and bleeding during and after sex. The extent to which these strategies reduced infection may need further research. What is important is that the women at least tried to do something about their situation. On what they thought should be done about prostitution in Zimbabwe, the women suggested that the government should empower them economically by funding income-generating projects for women. They further suggested that quality female and male condoms should be given to prostitutes for free.

Conclusion

This paper notes that prostitution in rural Zimbabwe is an arrangement for living which suits the income-generating capacities of women in particular circumstances. My research has shown a link between prostitution and poverty, especially among single mothers who lack the skills and resources to survive in ways that society considers dignified. It is also a product of a patriarchal morality designed to satisfy male sexuality without making men responsible for the outcomes of their sexual exploits.

The fact that most rural prostitutes are single mothers has serious implications. The more children a prostitute has, the poorer she becomes and the more she needs to continue in the sex trade to support herself and her children. The prostitutes' daughters in turn were likely to become prostitutes after learning the survival strategies of their mothers. We have already seen one fifteen-year-old girl, whose mother was a prostitute, resorting to prostitution. The fact that some prostitutes in rural Zimbabwe are girls below the age of sexual consent (sixteen years) may have serious implications for child welfare and the general health of the nation as these children may be infected with AIDS. As pointed out by the headman, prostitution may also have a negative impact on agricultural production as some people succumb to AIDS and others prefer to loiter around bars rather than to work in the fields.

We also saw that prostitutes had permanent boyfriends with husband-like roles. This ability to take both prostitute and wife-like roles illustrated their versatility in meeting the challenges of the sexual market as well as societal expectations. The fact that prostitutes played these double roles showed that they wanted to enjoy the benefits of both prostitution and marriage. It also showed that prostitutes, despite their profession, still uphold the societal values of marriage.

My data also show that prostitutes were vulnerable to HIV-infection due to the contradictions between the sexual needs of clients and the economic needs of sex workers. Desperate prostitutes in particular could not enforce the use of condoms because economic considerations took priority over long-term health benefits. Thus it can be argued that good health is not only a function of knowledge but also of resources. The respondents knew about STDs but could do little to avoid infection due to poverty and other constraints related to sex work.

Prostitutes' suggestions that the government could assist them by starting income-generating projects and by giving them condoms for free make sense in the context of a dysfunctional social welfare system. The latter suggestion requires that the government recognises prostitution as a legitimate form of livelihood and makes appropriate policy adjustments for this purpose. Unfortunately, this is unlikely considering societal attitudes towards prostitutes as displayed by the headman. Their suggestion to make divorce difficult for people with children may increase the misery of people locked in unhappy relationships. Perhaps the government could do more by ensuring that maintenance laws are strictly observed.

Chapter 7

Women and Millet Processing in Nyamadzawo Village

Stanford Mahati and Michael Bourdillon

Department of Sociology, University of Zimbabwe

New technologies have been developed to help women process their grain. In Nyamadzawo village near the Nyanyadzi irrigation scheme, women sometimes reject these technologies in favour of more cumbersome traditional methods for a variety of social and economic reasons. Here, we examine the need to see technology in the context in which it is to be used, and to understand the reasons why different actors make their various choices. This chapter is part of a larger study by Stanford Mahati on food processing and food security, based on fieldwork in the village from July 1998 to May 1999. The research collected detailed case material through participant observation and solicited views from a wide range of villagers.

About 70 per cent of Zimbabweans live in agriculturally marginal parts of the country and are dependent on agriculture for both food and income.[1] Food is a continuous priority in the rural areas although Zimbabwe as a whole produces a substantial food surplus. Africa's rulers have focused their attention on cities, where ordinary people sought economic opportunity and an escape from the drudgery and dullness of the rural areas.[2] What little attention agriculture has received has focused, more often than not, on cash crops for export rather than on staple food crops for local consumption.[3] Research into small-scale food processing by rural

---

[1] L. M. Zinyama, 'Local farmer organizations and rural development in Zimbabwe', in D. R. F. Taylor and F. McKenzie (eds), *Development from Within: Survival in Rural Africa*, Routledge, London, 1992.

[2] H. R. Davies, Jr, 'Agriculture, food and the colonial period', in A. Hansen and D. E. McMillan (eds), *Food in Sub-Saharan Africa*, Lynne Rienner Publishers, Colorado, 1986, p. 165.

[3] P. C. Timmer, 'Food security strategies: The Asian experience', FAO Agricultural Policy and Economic Development Series, No. 3, Rome, 1997.

families in communal lands, which is vital to household food security, has largely been neglected. Oesch[4] observed that for many decades traditional practices and ways of life were despised while development was sought by means of 'modern' methods and strategies. Only in recent years, when it became obvious that these modern ways had failed to bring about development in Africa, have policy-makers and planners turned to 'tradition'. This sector needs to be strengthened to promote food security through developing relevant technologies and changing negative attitudes towards traditionally processed foods.

Emphasis is on increasing productivity and reducing labour. Technology, widely seen as a panacea by the modernization school, is being introduced without due regard to social considerations. Technology is not value-neutral since it is understood, acquired and used on the basis of socio-economic relationships. Different people choose different processing technologies, and this needs to be investigated since it affects the fulfilment of objectives. Much remains to be learned about the level of utilization of new technology.

Women make a considerable contribution to agriculture in Africa. Development of sustainable rural livelihoods cannot be pursued without understanding the scope of women's activities and problems. The drudgery of women's work in agricultural activities provides a justification for the introduction of labour-saving devices and technological innovation for productivity in agriculture. Furthermore, Hahn pointed out that better processing methods generally improve life-styles by ensuring higher processing efficiency:[5] Madovi[6] mentioned that the labour-intensive problems associated with traditional technology are 'likely to disappear as mechanical or better methods of food preparation are introduced'. In Nyamadzawo Village however, the recently-introduced 'appropriate technology' in grain processing has some shortcomings.

If we are to understand the reasons behind choices in growing and processing millet, we need to place the choices in their contexts of the social structures and social processes in which they take place. In the research, attention was given to the perspectives of the participants, which inform the choices they make. Any

---

[4]   C. Oesch, 'Coping with the effects of drought: peasant strategies and government policy. The case of Zimbabwe's communal areas', diploma dissertation, Graduate Institute of Developmental Studies, Geneva, 1993, p. 1.

[5]   Cited by D. O'Neil, 'An improved stove for gari processing at the Asokwa Co-operative in Kumasi', Silsoe Research Institute, UK, 1999.

[6]   P. B. Madovi, *Food Handling in Shona Villages of Zimbabwe*, Gordon and Breach Science Publishers, United Kingdom, 1981, p. 134.

meaningful development in food processing will depend on these perspectives and the choices resulting from them.

Millet, described by Chinsman[7] as a 'poor man's crop', is grown and processed as a subsistence crop for local consumption. It is generally regarded as an inferior cereal when consumed as food.[8] Nevertheless, millet is a 'high-energy, nutritious food, especially recommended for children, convalescents and the elderly'.[9] This study concentrated only on pearl millet (*Pennisetum glaucum* or *mhunga*). It is the most important species of millet in Nyanyadzi both in terms of cropped area and contributions to food security.

Nyamadzawo Village

Nyamadzawo village is situated near Nyanyadzi business centre, 100 kilometres south of Mutare on the Mutare-Birchenough Bridge road. The dominant means of economic production is irrigation agriculture. The irrigation scheme is officially named Nyanyadzi after the river from which water was drawn.

The area has less than 650 millimetres of rain per year, and is subject to severe seasonal droughts. Officially, it is considered suitable only for extensive livestock and game ranching, supplemented by the cultivation of drought-resistant small grains such as millet and sorghum. Only the three largest rivers in the area, the Save, the Odzi and the Nyanyadzi continue to flow throughout the year. The dry land soils are shallow, coarse in texture and possess weak horizon development. These characteristics make them generally infertile and highly susceptible to erosion. All the vegetation in the Nyanyadzi area is adapted to low moisture and drought conditions. The drought resistant baobab tree (*Adansonia digitata*), which is a source of both food and livelihood, is abundant.

---

7   B. Chinsman, 'Choice of technique in sorghum and millet hulling in Africa', proceedings of ICC 11 Congress, Vienna, Austria, 1984, p. 3.

8   P. Chigumira noted that traditionally, the poor have grown millet and other small grains because they are drought-resistant and can be used to brew beer for sale. He argues that because maize has been regarded as a crop for richer people, consumers must be educated to accept small products, P. Chigumira, in M. I. Gomez, et al., 'Utilization of Sorghum and Millets', ICRISAT, Andhra Pradesh, 1992, p. 93.

9   FAO and ICRISAT, 'The world sorghum and millet economics: Facts, trends and outlook', a joint study by the Basic Foodstuffs Service, FAO Commodities and Trade Division and the Socio-economics and Policy Division, International Crops Research Institute for the Semi-Arid Tropics (ICRISAT), India and Rome, 1996, p. 40.

Nyamadzawo village is densely populated, with about 1,500 people at the time of research. The villagers have diverse social and cultural backgrounds. They are predominantly of the Ndau ethnic group. Members of this group call themselves the people of the *gova*, that is, the dry river valley.[10]

Mr Aron Kureketa, Village Head Makutamo and other elderly people reported that people had emigrated from the arid lands on which they had been settled by the white colonial government through their policy of land segregation.[11] People came to Nyanyadzi from areas like Shinja, Bikita, Mhakwe and Chipinge, hoping to get better farming and working opportunities in the irrigation scheme. Nyamadzawo village has a traditional patriarchal kinship system. The close-knit family units, although they are increasingly weakening, are vital for the survival of the community.

In August 1998, only a quarter of Nyamadzawo villagers owned land in the irrigation scheme. The remaining 75 per cent are either dry-land farmers or tenant farmers in the irrigation scheme. The yields in the dry lands are low in most years and consequently the demand for land in the more dependable irrigation scheme is high. Besides, land suitable for agriculture is becoming increasingly scarce.[12]

Dry-land farmers obtain cash by selling agricultural produce, working as non-plot holders in the irrigation scheme, doing piece work in the village, receiving remittances, trading within the village, and selling baobab artefacts to tourists and traders (see chapters 4 and 5 in this volume). People are continuously in search of cash for several reasons, especially for food, agricultural inputs, school fees, medical care and milling money. Women and children[13] are the ones who usually cover such costs and they work continuously on irrigated plots, dry lands or gardens.

---

[10] C. Vijfhuizen, 'The people you live with: Gender identities and social practices, beliefs and power in the livelihoods of the Ndau women and men in a village with an irrigation scheme in Zimbabwe', Ph.D. thesis, the University of Wageningen, 1998, p. 17.

[11] K. M. Mutowo writes that the people in the Sabi Valley, in which Nyanyadzi is situated, suffered from chronic food shortages even before the enactment of the Land Apportionment Act of 1930 because of earlier land alienation that had deprived them of fertile soils, K. M. Mutowo, 'Nyanyadzi Irrigation Scheme: Origin and Development (1936-1965)', B. A. dissertation, Department of Economic History, University of Zimbabwe, 1987, p. 7.

[12] In Zimbabwe 67 per cent of all the communal areas have already exceeded their recommended carrying capacity, FAO, *Agricultural Services Bulletin*, No. 89, 1991, p. 13.

[13] For case studies of child workers in Nyanyadzi see Y. Chirwa and M. F. C. Bourdillon, 'Small-scale commercial farming: Working children in Nyanyadzi irrigation scheme', in M. F. C. Bourdillon (ed.), *Earning a Life: Working Children in Zimbabwe*, Weaver Press, Harare, 2000, pp. 127-145.

Processing millet

Three cereal grains of importance are grown in Nyamadzawo village: millet, sorghum and maize. While wheat is also important in consumption, only irrigation farmers grow and process it. This study focuses on millet, with some comment on sorghum, since the processing of these small grains is similar.

In Nyanyadzi, where food is scarce, cereals play a vital role in contributing to household food security and to the nutritional intake of dry-land farmers. Carbohydrates and proteins are the two main constituents by weight in any grain and they offer, after water, the two most important substances for survival, energy and protein.[14] Farmers use both traditional and new processing technologies to clean, dehull, and grind the grains into flour. We review traditional and new technologies for dehulling and grinding, and discuss the effectiveness and utilization of these technologies by different rural people.

There are many reasons why sorghum and pearl millet are important. Unlike maize and wheat, which require fertile soils and relatively high levels of rainfall, small grains thrive under less than ideal soil and climatic conditions. The small, drought-resistant grains are increasingly being given importance by African policy-makers who are concerned with national cereal self-sufficiency, household food security and the need to widen their nation's cereal base.[15] In marginal areas of Zimbabwe, production of sorghum and millet is essential. These grains have good nutritional value, probably because they are generally consumed in a less-refined form than other cereals.

Although the small grains are widely used for human consumption in the communal areas, intensive processing methods are far from adequate. In most cases, machines designed for other cereals such as maize, rice and wheat have been adapted for the small grains.[16] In Zimbabwe, the small grains are usually processed using dehullers and mills that were specifically designed for maize.

---

14   UNIFEM, 'Cereal Processing', Food Cycle Technology Source Book, No. 3, United Nations Development Fund for Women, New York, 1988, p. 8.
15   K. Mazvimavi, 'Economic analysis of the competitive position of sorghum and millet in semi-arid, smallholder farming regions of Zimbabwe', unpublished M.Phil. thesis, University of Zimbabwe, 1996; B. Hedden-Dunkhorst, 'The contribution of sorghum and millet versus maize to food security in semi-arid Zimbabwe', unpublished D.Phil. thesis, University of Hohenheim, 1993; M. W. Bassey and O. G. Schmidt, *Abrasive-disk Dehullers in Africa: From Research to Dissemination*, IDRC, Ottawa, 1989, p. 1.
16   FAO, 'Post-harvest and processing technologies for African staple foods: A technical compendium', *Agricultural Services Bulletin*, No. 89, Rome, 1991.

Pearl millet undergoes a number of processes that are arduous and time-consuming prior to milling (see Figure 1). This section outlines the steps involved in both traditional and improved technologies of processing millet by the dry-land farmers of Nyanyadzi. In this study we consider the preparation of millet grain after harvesting for immediate and long-term consumption, using both traditional and new technology.

Figure 1: Steps involved in traditional and improved technologies of processing millet.

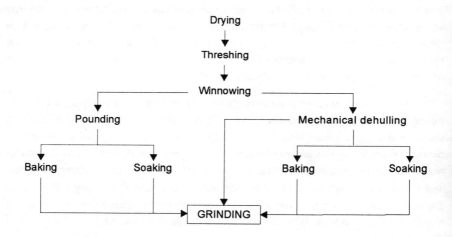

In brief, after the millet is dried in the sun, it is threshed and winnowed. Villagers, usually women, then dehull the millet by pounding in the traditional method or using machines. After pounding the millet, some prefer to process it further according to tradition either by baking or by soaking the millet in water. The millet is finally ground into meal for *sadza* (thick porridge), *bota* (a thin porridge) and yeast for brewing purposes.

The introduction of new technology in the processing of millet has raised a number of problems. The substitution of traditional methods, which are time-consuming and laborious, with new technology, which is claimed to be more efficient, has negatively affected the taste and quality of the meal. Furthermore, the new technology is not affordable to all in the rural areas. This is a paradox, given that the new technology is supposed to promote food security.

Threshing and winnowing

Harvested millet is first sun-dried on a raised stand. It remains on the stand during harvesting time to ensure that it does not germinate if rain falls. Women have to be constantly on the watch and ready to bring the cereal under cover in the case of sudden showers in order to avoid loss by spoilage and increased grain breakage on milling. Between February and early April 1999, most women had difficulties in removing drying grain and many households experienced some grain losses.

It is also necessary for the grain to be guarded from birds while drying. This task is not arduous, but it is time-consuming and falls to women and children. Although many use mechanical pest-scaring devices that do not interfere with other light domestic duties, these are not very effective and little can substitute for traditional bird-scaring by women and children

When the millet is drying, women prepare a floor, surfaced with cow dung and earth, called the *mbuva*. The millet is spread on the *mbuva* to dry and turned over periodically. The millet is threshed on the *mbuva* to separate the kernel from the stalk, using sticks approximately 1.5 metres long and three centimetres in diameter. The manual threshing method is very simple and cheap but very laborious. At the start of the threshing period, most of the villagers developed blisters on their hands.

The threshing process produces fine dust that irritates the skin. Most villagers reported that the new hybrid millet introduced by agricultural scientists has dust that makes them itch more than the traditional millet. For this reason, some growers prefer the old varieties, although the new varieties produce more grain and have a longer shelf life.[17]

Threshing the millet on the floor allows impurities to be mixed with the grain, which later cause grinding and eating problems. To minimize impurities the women had continuously to re-surface the *mbuva* with cow-dung. Modern threshing machines have been developed which can do the work efficiently.[18] However, in Nyamadzawo village and the surrounding areas, there was no one with a hand-driven thresher or a powered thresher. The villagers reported that the modern

---

[17] In other areas, farmers have rejected new, semi-dwarf varieties of millet and sorghum because the long stems of traditional varieties are used for building materials, C. Hiebsch and K. S. O'Hair, 'Major domesticated food crops', in A. Hansen and D. E. McMillan (eds), *Food in Sub-Saharan Africa*, Lynne Rienner Publishers, Colorado, 1986, p. 186.

[18] UNIFEM, 'Cereal Processing', Food Cycle Technology Source Book, No. 3, United Nations Development Fund for Women, New York, 1988.

threshers were out of their price-range, especially as they do not have credit facilities. In September 2000, ENDA-Zimbabwe was selling a seven horse power sorghum thresher with a petrol engine but without the mortar at $50,700 (US$920).

The next step in the processing of millet is winnowing to separate chaff from the grain. Soil, small stones and trash (such as empty grains) are also removed. Separating impurities from threshed grain requires almost as much labour as threshing. The traditional method of winnowing, which is used in the village, requires much patience and the presence of suitable wind. It is only women who winnow grain, and preferably skilled and experienced women to minimize losses. The lighter chaff and straw are blown away while the heavy grains fall more or less vertically.

Finally, the grain is cleaned with a winnowing basket that is shaken until chaff and dust separate at the upper edge. The process is usually repeated frequently before the grain is satisfactorily cleaned. Apart from improving millet's palatability and nutritional value, removal of dust and other foreign material reduces the tendency of grain to heat in storage.[19]

Dehulling and grinding

Dehulling is the process of removing the outer coat of the grain, which is the source of the bitter taste (polyphenols or tanning) often found in the outer hull or in the testa layer immediately under it.[20] There are two methods of dehulling millet applied in the village: the traditional manual method and the use of mechanical dehullers, recently introduced but becoming common. Socio-economic conditions influence the people in their choice of method.

In traditional dehulling, the millet is pounded using a wooden pestle and mortar. The grain is put into a mortar with a bit of water and pounded until the bran is separated. The pounding and winnowing processes are repeated several times before good quality millet flour is obtained. One woman reported that failure to do the work thoroughly would make the sadza bitter to eat to such an extent that 'one who is very hungry would not even eat the sadza'.

Hand pounding is time-consuming, tedious and labour-intensive. Two women can produce around 2.5 kilogrammes in one and a half hours. Thus to produce a

---

[19] FAO, 'Processing and storage of foodgrains by rural families', *Agricultural Services Bulletin*, No. 53, Rome, 1983, p. 22.
[20] M. W. Bassey and O. G. Schmidt, *Abrasive-Disk Dehullers in Africa: From Research to Dissemination*, IDRC, Ottawa, 1989, p. 3.

good product the job needs to be done by healthy personnel. Inexperienced women, and especially young orphans, find it very difficult to dehull the family's daily requirements. People suffering from AIDS are abandoning the growing and processing of millet, thus exposing themselves to food insecurity.

Another disadvantage of traditional processing methods is the incomplete dehulling of the bran, which affects the taste of the porridge produced.[21] Further hand pounding by unskilled people can result in a high degree of grain breakage. The conditions under which the flour is produced tend to be unhygienic especially in this area where water is scarce for most households.

Women preferred pounding grain at home during times of food scarcity and when they have low food reserves. Pounding at home is economical and ensures food availability in the household. For example, in a household of six people eating two meals a day, a bucket of millet meal processed traditionally will last about two weeks. On the other hand, if the mechanical dehullers process the bucket, the bucket of flour would not last two weeks: *'hupfu hwacho hunofamba'.* Approximately one fifth of a bucket of bran is removed after traditionally dehulling a bucket of millet. Usually when the grains are dehulled manually, the bran is not completely extracted. However, nearly two fifths of a bucket of bran is lost through mechanical dehulling. Mechanical dehullers are very effective in removing bran, which consequently leads to a reduction in the quality and quantity of the output.[22]

Technologists generally regard the introduction of mechanical dehullers as a useful development in the rural areas.[23] They argue that dehullers are an appropriate technological response to the time-consuming rural methods of hand pounding millet, sorghum, maize and other grains. Mechanical processing of small grains can release up to four or five hours of women and children's time per day. This time could be used on activities such as knitting, sewing, gardening, studying and housekeeping.

The dehullers scrape away the hull of the grain by the grinding action of whirling stones and the friction of other grains. The rate of flow of the grain is

---

[21] K. Mazvimavi, 'Economic analysis of the competitive position of sorghum and millet in semi-arid, smallholder farming regions of Zimbabwe', unpublished M.Phil. thesis, University of Zimbabwe, 1996.

[22] K. Mazvimavi confirmed that bran is not completely extracted in manual dehulling. He also noted that about fifteen per cent of the grain, by weight, is lost as bran in mechanical dehulling. In practice the loss is likely to be higher since he did not take into account lack of proper training by the millers and their deliberate use of wrong sieves in order to maximize profits, ibid., p. 63.

[23] A Zimbabwean non-governmental organization, Environmental Development Activities (ENDA-Zimbabwe) introduced the Mini-ENDA dehuller and initiated a dehuller dissemination campaign, M. I. Gomez, *et al.*, 'Utilization of Sorghum and Millets', ICRISAT, Andhra Pradesh, 1992, p. 12.

adjusted by the miller so that the grain is kept in the casing just long enough to remove the desired amount of bran. The lighter bran is continually removed from the dehulled grain by a fan.[24] This mechanical method is known as 'dry abrasion' because water is not added to the grain at any stage of processing.

The mechanical dehullers work at a high speed and are capable of producing in five to ten minutes dehulled grain that would take women from two to five hours to complete under the traditional pestle and mortar method. Mechanical dehulling, however, is expensive, especially for crops like millet and sorghum.

Moreover, 70 per cent of the consumers find it awkward to carry home a separate container of bran, and consequently leave their bran instead of feeding it to their chickens. The millers get the bran free or cheaply ($2.50 a bucket) and later sell it in bulk at around $50 (US$1.30) a bag (about four buckets) to St Patrick's Mission School, two kilometres away.

The following case study of Paidamoyo Grinding Mill shows some of the reasons behind the use of the dehullers and the efforts made by some millers to help their customers.

Paidamoyo Grinding Mill

Paidamoyo Grinding Mill is located at the Nyanyadzi Service Centre. Its catchment area includes Gudyanga, Tonhorai, Nenhowe, Nemaramba and some areas in the Buhera District just across the Save River. The dehuller was not very much in use from August 1998 to early February 1999 as the people were experiencing acute grain shortage. The dehullers were considered by customers to be very wasteful and expensive. From late February 1999 to July 1999, the demand for the dehuller's service was high because, as Edmore Chiwora, the miller, explained, 'people had a bumper harvest both in the irrigation schemes and in the dry-lands'.

The milling price is continually increasing. On many occasions, the miller has impounded buckets of mealie-meal from desperate customers after they failed to pay for the services. However, after listening to the pleas of poor clients, he has several times given clients their grain on the understanding that they would pay soon. The owner of the grinding mill does not like this practice because many times he has been forced to write off debts. He said, 'It is difficult to impound customers' grain because I live in the same community with them and above all, I am related to some of them ... The result is that we make some losses.'

---

24   UNIFEM, 'Cereal Processing', Food Cycle Technology Source Book, No. 3, United Nations Development Fund for Women, New York, 1988, p. 25.

During public holidays, Paidamoyo Grinding Mill charges special low prices. The owner says this is 'to ease people's monetary problems'. In August 1999, the normal prices for dehulling and grinding millet were $10 and $8 per bucket respectively. During the Heroes Day holiday in August 1999, the price was reduced by $3 across the board.

As a free service to customers who live far away, every Friday between April and August, the workers at the grinding mill visit grain collection centres at Gudyanga, Tonhorai, Nenhowe and Chikwizi to collect grain for grinding. This customer service does not cover the period from August to March, as only a few customers are willing to dehull maize grain. At Paidamoyo Grinding Mill, when fixing a fee, the miller takes into account the actual quantity of grain after dehulling. For example, dehulling millet costs $10 per bucket and grinding $8 per bucket. After dehulling, a bucket of millet will be only three-quarters full. Paidamoyo then only charges $7.50 instead of the full price of $8, whilst other millers make no such reduction.

The dehulled millet is ground into meal at the milling place or taken home for further traditional processing between dehulling and grinding. There is a problem in that the grinding mills are neither accessible nor centrally located. Most of the houses in the village are located at least two kilometres from the mills. Some villagers walk or travel by bus more than ten kilometres to use the dehullers. This hinders the adoption of new technology, especially by those who want to bake or soak the dehulled millet between dehulling and grinding, but who resent visiting the distant grinding mills twice to complete the processing.

Optional traditional processing

After the millet has been dehulled either manually or mechanically, the popular traditional method of processing millet in Nyamadzawo is to bake the grain. People bake millet for three reasons. First, baking enhances the flavour of the millet meal: the *sadza* becomes more palatable. Second, people say the *sadza* will not get cold quickly after it has been cooked, thus saving firewood for heating. Third, preservation is achieved by heat during baking. The low moisture content inhibits the growth of bacteria when the grain is ground into flour and thus prolongs shelf life.

Two to three kilogrammes of millet are put into clay pots 300 to 400 millimetres wide. The woman sits sideways by the fire and continuously turns the millet in the pot with the right or left hand. To process a bucket of millet generally takes an hour and a half. The process is stopped when the millet produces a certain good smell. Judging the point at which baking is complete is a subjective matter, depending largely on the experience and skill of the baker. Often children and other inexperienced young adults over-heat the millet, resulting in the *sadza* not tasting good.

The disadvantage of baking is that the constant stirring of millet grain over a fire requires the processor to endure heat and smoke for lengthy periods. Furthermore, the villagers faced the problem of getting firewood: Nyanyadzi has suffered major deforestation and both traditional and government authorities strictly prohibit cutting trees.

The second and less popular method of processing dehulled millet is to soak the millet in water for about 24 hours. If the millet is soaked for too long the product will have a strong sour taste. Both over- and under-fermentation badly affect the texture of the product. The millet is made to ferment to give the *sadza* a unique good taste, 'slippery texture', and many reported that it becomes very nutritious.[25] During fermenting, sand and stones are removed through sedimentation. This also improves the quality of the *sadza*.

The wet millet is dried[26] on clean reed mats or sacks. Finally, the millet is ground into meal. However, the millet must not be too dry or wet when it is sent to the grinding mill. If wet, the millet blocks the sieves. If the millet is very dry, the flour will not be very fine.

These two treatments affect the taste of the meal differently. While indigenous people prefer to bake their millet, immigrants from neighbouring areas like Marange and Buhera like to soak it.

Organization of labour in millet processing

Women are the mainstays of rural food production and food processing is their domain. In Nyanyadzi, as elsewhere in the developing world, family meals are usually prepared by women, who are involved in the various stages of processing millet for consumption.

Although men appreciate the role of women in processing food, some beliefs make their task more difficult. For example, women who prepare the *mbuva* surface

---

[25] Beneficial bacteria, which are a by-product of fermentation, increase the acidity or alcohol content of the food and therefore prevent the growth of food poisoning bacteria, P. Fellows (ed.), *Traditional Foods: Processing for Profit*, Intermediate Technology Publications, London, 1997, p. 19.

[26] The main purpose of drying is to preserve foods by removing the water that is needed for microbial growth and enzyme activity, ibid., p. 16.

with cow-dung are not allowed to enter the cattle *kraals*. There is a belief that if women enter the *kraal*, especially those of childbearing age, they bring a bad omen and the cattle will fail to reproduce or to produce enough milk. In many households, only young girls, old women and males are allowed to enter a *kraal*. Often work to surface the *mbuva* was delayed as women waited for men or young girls to collect cow-dung.

Traditionally, any member of the family, regardless of sex and age, can participate in threshing. In most cases, however, women work alone, since their husbands and children are away from home. Children as young as seven thresh sorghum or millet after school, during holidays and weekends. In our study, Shingirai Sithole, aged seven, participated in threshing millet. His mother argued that 'he has to work because he wants to eat'.

In the past, relatives and some friendly neighbours helped with processing, either in groups or individually. Among the Shona, these labour groups are called *nhimbe*. Labour was exchanged for traditional beer and sometimes produce. Such labour groups were mainly utilized when extra labour was needed, such as during land preparation and harvesting and in some stages of food processing. The labour groups were very helpful to the aged, young and small households. Furthermore, working together is an expression of social solidarity. This served further to strengthen kinship ties and food exchange networks. Now the villagers are no longer willing to work for beer, and prefer contract labour for cash.

The practice of working in *nhimbe* has further been discouraged because many people expect to be given some of the produce in appreciation for their work. However, people cannot afford to give a helper half a bucket of grain if less than six buckets have been harvested. Failure to reward people well for their help leads to strained relationships, and disgruntled helpers would snub any call for assistance the next season. Since a harvest is barely enough to meet one family's demand for a full year, people worked as family units without inviting outside help.

Women, at times assisted by children of both sexes, sometimes as young as nine, pound grain using a pestle and mortar. However, boys around the age of sixteen refuse to pound arguing that it is 'women's work'. Girls have no way of opting out. In Nyamadzawo, older women usually winnow the grain because of their skill.

Mr Gudyanga, aged 45 and a father of four children, sympathizes with his wife and children when he sees them pounding grain. He feels 'as if I am punishing my family'. Occasionally when he has little money, he has the grain, especially millet, mechanically dehulled.

The decision on whether to soak or bake millet is usually made by women. Men understand that it is the responsibility of women to decide what is good for the family. Pearson Mutezo explained that men could not complain much about the quality of the meal because they are not the ones who do the difficult processing work. Women perform these tasks in most cases because they do not have money and they want to please their husbands.

Partly because of the problems in processing, women, especially the young and educated, decide against planting millet and prefer instead to plant more maize despite an increased risk of crop failure because of erratic and low rainfall. Maize is perceived to be more palatable than millet.

Apart from their work in processing grain, women, with the help of children, have to guard drying grain against pests and against spoiling from rain.

New or traditional technologies

The following case studies illustrate the reasons why people are utilizing the new technologies, and why some people have not fully adopted them.

Grandmother Mahaka

Grandmother Mahaka, aged 64, is divorced and lives alone. She grows sorghum and millet on two acres of land at her homestead. Although experienced in the pounding of grain, she welcomed the introduction of mechanical dehullers. She said, 'Takomborerwa chembere.' (We the old ladies are now blessed.) She argued that old age forces her to embrace the new technology.

She pointed out that manually pounding millet is not wasteful as women take great care in minimizing grain wastage. Contrary to the widespread belief that the quality of mechanically dehulled flour is better than flour that has been pounded manually, Mrs Mahaka maintained that the quality of flour she pounds at home is better. Several villagers concurred with her sentiments. She argued that she was very thorough. Like many others in the villages, Mrs Mahaka uses the mechanical dehullers when she is not feeling well and when her harvest is very good.

After mechanically dehulling the millet, she always takes the grain home to bake it. She likes to bake the millet because she grew up using this method. Although taking the dehulled grain to her house, which is about three kilometres from the dehullers, is extra work, she regularly does that. Mrs Mahaka cannot stomach the idea of eating *sadza* made from unbaked millet. She pointed out that the mechanical dehullers are good but she called for the introduction of dehullers that can replace the traditional processes of baking or soaking millet.

Grandmother Bingepinge

Mrs Bingepinge is in her late 60s and prefers to dehull her grain (maize, sorghum or millet) with the mechanical dehullers whenever she can afford it. She challenged me, 'I would like to see how much you would dehull using mortar and pestle if I give you a bucket. I am no longer able to pound.'

After dehulling maize, she immediately winnows it at the milling place and has the dehulled grain ground. With millet however, she has no option despite her advanced age and ill-health but to carry the dehulled millet home for baking. Her house is situated about two kilometres from the Service Centre. At home, before baking the dehulled millet, she thoroughly cleans and winnows the grain. The mechanical dehullers can only winnow wheat, rice and maize, not millet and sorghum. One miller explained that this is because '*chinoremerwa*' (millet and sorghum are too heavy to be winnowed by dehullers). Consequently, even those who do not want to bake or soak millet have to manually winnow the dehulled millet at the grinding place before the grain is finally mechanically ground.

Like others in the village, Mrs Bingepinge has abandoned the laborious traditional method of grinding dehulled grain into meal flour using one small flat stone on a larger one. The mechanical grinders are used despite the fact that they are far away and their prices for grinding prohibitive for many people. Like other women, Mrs Bingepinge uses the grinding stones when she wants a small quantity of flour for *mahewu*, the traditional soft drink.

Mrs Bingepinge reported that once she was forced to pay $20 (US 76c) for repairing a damaged sieve. The miller had claimed that her grain had some stones, which damaged the sieve. She was not sure whether the actual cost of repairing the sieve was $20 or less. On many occasions due to transport problems and because she cannot afford to buy a sack she either loses the bran or sells it at the give-away price of $1.50 a bucket.

Mrs Nechipote

Mrs Nechipote is a widow aged 33, who has five young children. Her husband died in 1996. She inherited from her husband an acre in the dry lands. Together with her family, she regularly works in the Nyanyadzi Irrigation Scheme for a small fee to make ends meet. Mrs Nechipote was raised in Nyanga, where she was used to growing maize rather than millet. She only started to grow millet in 1985, when she married and settled in Nyanyadzi.

From 1985 to 1997, she grew millet on a large portion of her land. She and her husband used to rent two acres of dry land. In the 1997-98 season, she decided to abandon growing millet on a large scale, mainly because the work that is required to grow and process millet is too much for her alone. In 1996-97 season, she had failed to cope with the work involved in harvesting and processing millet. This resulted in her losing about four buckets to persistent rains.

Furthermore, her children expressed strong reservations against eating millet *sadza*. She now prefers to use half of her field to grow sorghum, which is easier to process than millet. Mrs Nechipote prefers to use the dehullers when processing millet instead of using the pestle and mortar because she says the latter method is difficult. Above all, she does not have time to pound millet as she has to run her household and work in the irrigation scheme for money.

After dehulling the millet, she prefers to grind the millet immediately into meal instead of taking the dehulled grain home for baking. She does not have the energy and time for this. However, she complained bitterly that she has no control over the dehulling of her millet. Most of the time she felt exploited by the millers.

The different tasks in processing millet are often arduous, monotonous and time-consuming, and the introduction of new technology has generally been welcomed. However, traditionalists and conservatives, who are mainly elderly people, are very critical about this development. This can be seen in the cases of Mrs Mahaka and Mrs Bingepinge, who continue to bake millet.

Apart from the problems of labour in processing millet, there are also problems of taste. Despite great efforts to remove sand from the millet or sorghum, the *sadza* will always contain some grains of sand. People say that these can cause constipation, especially in very young children and the ill. Furthermore, the grey-purplish colour of millet *sadza* makes it less appealing especially to children, visitors and immigrants who are used to eating white *sadza*. To overcome the problem of colour and constipation, the locals mix the millet or sorghum flour with white maize meal.

Elderly women argued that young women have neither the patience to process millet traditionally nor the will to work hard for a good taste. Although the young women acknowledged that millet processed in the traditional way tastes better, they said that the value and taste of *sadza* which has not been soaked and baked earlier is of secondary importance to them.

The traditionalists, who include elderly men, argued against the adoption of new technologies, saying that they detracted from some aspects of Shona culture. For example, daughters, daughters-in-law and mothers are expected to pound grain for ritual ceremonies. They are expected to be able to process grain thoroughly and properly. Failure by a daughter-in-law to do the tasks well shames her parents as this implies that they failed to socialize her. In the past, the daughter-in-law would be sent back to her parents for training in food processing. The traditionalists argued that by abandoning the use of mortar and pestle, Shona customs and practices were being lost.

The relationship between millers and customers

The lack of ownership or control over the use of modern technology by women and children has created socio-economic problems for the rural poor. Grain is reduced in quantity, the cost of using the machine is high, and the bran is lost.

Conditioning of grain to the correct moisture content prior to milling is important for good separation of the constituent parts. If grain is too dry it is hard, difficult to break down, and requires more energy to convert it to flour. If the grain is too moist, material tends to adhere to machine surfaces and prevent efficient screening. In both cases flour yields and quality are affected. The problem the customers face is how to determine the appropriate moisture content to produce maximum results. Most farmers can judge if the grain is dry enough to grind, for example by pressing the kernel with the thumbnail or crushing it between the teeth. Nevertheless, assessing the moisture content of the grain is very subjective. In February 1999, many people walked long distances only to be turned away after millers judged the moisture content of their grain to be too high. This was at a time when most of the households had no grain to eat.

There are no regulations about the required content of nutrients in food after milling. Stewart and Amerine[27] argued that all the steps employed in the processing and preservation of food have an impact on its nutritive value. Some

---

[27] F. G. Stewart, and M. A. Amerine, *Food Science and Technology: A Series of Monographs*, Academic Press, New York, 1973. p. 131.

may improve it, but most have adverse effects. The nutrient losses that occur during the handling, processing, and storing of foods largely involve the vitamins and minerals. In Nyamadzawo, probably the greatest loss, and one regretted by most villagers, is the removal of nutrients by mechanical dehullers. This is related to loss of volume. Since white *sadza* is the preferred product, machines that remove much bran, germ and other non-endosperm layers are very popular among the villagers. Consequently, the nutritive value of the *sadza* has progressively declined. People who are unwell or aged and who drop traditional methods of food processing for want of energy have the greatest need of the full nutritional value of the meal. None of the millers at Nyanyadzi are properly trained to control nutrition losses. Their job is to determine simply that the grain has been adequately milled.

Villagers prefer very fine flour that lasts longer in storage and is easy to cook. Two factors control the fineness of the flour: the sieve aperture and the speed at which the grain is put through the machine.

If the miller puts grain in the milling machine rapidly, the resulting meal is coarse. Attempts by customers to control the rate of putting the grain into the mill often resulted in conflict with the millers. Some millers stubbornly refused to do what the customers wanted. The problem was worse for customers who sent their children to the milling place. Children ended up taking low quality flour, as they were powerless to argue with the miller.

The 'zero sieve' produces very fine flour whilst the 'one sieve' has larger pores that produce a coarser flour. Because the 'one sieve' is faster and uses less electricity, millers usually want to use this sieve, especially when there are many people wanting to grind grain. Most customers are either not free to select the type of sieve to be used or are ignorant about the types of sieves to use for each particular grain.

Millers are often slow to replace a damaged sieve, resulting in poor texture of the meal. For example, one miller at Nyanyadzi took a week to replace a damaged sieve. Pleas by customers to have the sieve replaced were ignored. The miller finally repaired the sieve only after customers started boycotting his grinding-mill.

Another way millers sometimes try to save on electricity and cut expenses is to stop the grinding process early and then stop the machine from continuing to pour the flour into the sack. Many customers justifiably complained that they were being robbed of their flour.

Millers were often accused of cheating customers. This usually happened when children had been sent to the grinding mill. Inexperienced or malicious millers deliberately do not stop the dehuller in time to avoid over-dehulling. Over-dehulling leads to significant quantity reduction. In one incident, the lady complained that the grain had to be thoroughly dehulled. The miller reluctantly repeated the process. Unfortunately the lady forgot to tell the operator to stop the dehuller in time and the miller knowingly left the dehuller on. Her grain was over-dehulled and she lost half her bucket. Later in an interview with me, the miller said, 'We fix them if they order me to repeat the dehulling process when I am satisfied that the grain has been adequately dehulled.'

When there are long queues, the millers refuse to dehull millet and sorghum, as they want to serve as many customers as possible. Dehulling and grinding millet or sorghum takes longer than maize. In most cases customers with millet and sorghum are served last. Millers and some customers with maize argued against grinding millet or sorghum first because that spoils the colour of white maize meal. Furthermore, the millers pointed out that the grinders of dehullers wear out more quickly if used often to process millet and sorghum. Grinders are expensive to buy. Because of these problems, only one miller out of four at Nyanyadzi Service Centre regularly agrees to dehull sorghum and millet. Consequently, the customers do not benefit fully from the dehullers.

Conclusion

The introduction of new technology in the processing of millet has led to reduced workloads for many women. At the same time, a number of factors work against its full adoption. Conservative members of the community claim that the new technology undermines African traditional practices and culture. The technology also compromises quantity, taste and nutritional value of the food.

Although the introduction of new machines, which are operated only by men, did much to improve the quality of life of rural women, this has led to men taking over the important task of processing grain. Male millers are concerned with maximizing profits rather than the interests of customers. The FAO[28] argues that in such circumstances, it is usually preferable to encourage the introduction

---

[28] FAO, 'Processing and storage of foodgrains by rural families', *Agricultural Services Bulletin*, No. 53, Rome, 1983, p. 2.

of hand-operated machines that leave women in control but reduce their labour. This is not to imply that women can never manage and operate agricultural machinery. In Africa, there are many instances of powered threshers being run by women, with corresponding enhancement of their status.[29] If some women in Nyamadzawo could operate the machines, women would have more say in determining the quality and quantity of the flour. During this study, many women expressed the view that if there had been female millers their problems of quality and quantity control would have been better attended to.

Furthermore, the new technology is expensive and not very accessible to the rural poor. Only the rural elite uses the dehullers regularly. To improve life for poor people, new technologies are needed that are cheap, save time and require minimum labour, but at the same time are culturally acceptable and ensure that people continue to control how they are used.

The lack of an effective sorghum and millet-processing technology is a major constraint to the more widespread production and utilization of the small grains.[30] Traditional milling is still practised by smallholders and poor households because it is socially, technically and financially acceptable to users, who are usually women. A mechanical milling process controlled by customers and capable of producing meal cheaply, will likely lead away from over-dependence on maize and promote the consumption of pearl millet and sorghum that require small amounts of rainfall.

Although the introduction of the new technology was aimed at improving the lives of the rural poor, its impact has sadly been far from straightforward. The processing of millet remains labour-intensive since the new technology failed to incorporate some of the advantages of traditional processing millet. The introduction of relevant and appropriate technology should proceed firstly by identifying the advantages and disadvantages of existing or traditional technology, and secondly by screening preferred technologies. Then the most relevant or appropriate technology should be selected on the basis of its capacity to overcome the disadvantages of traditional technology. Negative attitudes towards the processing and consumption of millet or sorghum need to be changed to increase the utilization of these small grains, which do very well in this drought-prone area. The compliance of the new technology to socio-economic and technical demands should consequently lead to significant improvement of rural people's livelihoods.

---

29   Ibid.
30   B. Hedden-Dunkhost, 'The contribution of sorghum and millet versus maize to food security in semi-arid Zimbabwe', unpublished D.Phil. thesis, University of Hohenheim, 1993.

Chapter 8

In Search of a Better Life: Small-Scale Food Processors in Rusitu Valley and Murewa

Rose Machiridza and Emmanuel Manzungu

Department of Soil Sciences and Agricultural Engineering, University of Zimbabwe

Outside agents tried to 'open the eyes' of two groups of rural women in Zimbabwe, located in Rusitu Valley in Chipinge district and in Murewa district, to ways of improving their livelihoods through income-generating projects in the form of small-scale food processing.[1] However, the benefits did not meet expectations owing to problems with the technology when applied to the social settings of the women. This chapter illustrates the importance of the social dimensions of technology.

The aim of the intervention was to reduce poverty, which has reached endemic levels in the country and is threatening the lives of many people. Poverty is reported to be most prevalent in rural areas where about 70 per cent of Zimbabwe's total population reside.[2] In the early 1990s, 75 per cent of the households in the rural areas were classified as poor compared to 39 per cent in urban areas.[3] This

---

[1]   A fuller account of this research is presented in E. Manzungu *et al.*, 'An evaluation of small-scale fruit and vegetable drying in Murewa', report prepared for Ranche House College, 2000.

[2]   In recent years, poverty has been increasing in the urban areas.

[3]   According to GOZ's 1995 poverty assessment study survey, poverty is defined in economic terms as the inability to afford a defined basket of consumption items that are necessary to sustain life. Two poverty lines have been calculated, the Food Poverty Line (FPL) and the Total Consumption Poverty Line (TCPL). FPL gives the amount of income required to buy a basket of basic food needed by an average person per annum. This was calculated at $1,289.81. TCPL gives the amount of income required to purchase a basket of food and non-food (clothing, education, health, and transport) items by an average person per annum calculated at $2,132.33. The person whose income is below the FPL is very poor; below the TCPL and above the FPL is poor; above the TCPL is non-poor.

paper examines the efforts made to assist one of the most vulnerable groups of people in the country: women, who make up about 60 per cent of the population in rural areas and are reported to head most poor households.[4]

Poverty levels in the study areas are comparable to the rest of the country. Sixty-eight per cent of the population in Chipinge falls into the very poor category, thirteen per cent into the poor category and nineteen per cent into the non-poor category. A government report[5] noted that poverty was more prevalent among women and children with 77 per cent of the women in the very poor category compared to 57 per cent for men. Thirty per cent of the men were in the non-poor category compared to only nine per cent of the women.[6] Murewa District in Mashonaland East province was ranked the third poorest in the province with 84 per cent of the population in the poor category.[7] Taking only rural Murewa (excluding the administrative town), 73 per cent of the population was in the very poor category, fourteen per cent in the poor category and only thirteen per cent in the non-poor category.[8] These statistics established the case for the donor's intervention to alleviate poverty. We show in this paper, however, that such efforts to improve the livelihoods of people must be circumspect and take due cognizance of the particular circumstances of the people concerned.

The premise of the intervention was, according to the proponents, simple and straightforward. Women should be helped to exploit, to their advantage, the resources available to them. Murewa district has an abundance of mangoes while Rusitu Valley boasts bananas, oranges, pineapples, mangoes and guavas. However, the local fresh market for these fruits is limited. Marketing outside the production areas is hampered by poor road networks and a lack of transport. As a result, heavy losses are experienced, which reduce the potential income of the people in these areas. Small-scale food processing was seen to present a possible solution to the problem. Food processing preserves and modifies foods so as to make them safe, appealing and of uniform quality. It adds value to produce by extending shelf-life and reducing weight and bulk, making transport cheaper and storage easier. Our study in the distribution of dried fruits in Chitungwiza

[4]   GOZ, 'Poverty assessment study survey: Distribution of poverty in Zimbabwe', Ministry of Public Service, Labour and Social Welfare – Social Development Fund, 1995a, pp. 69-70.

[5]   GOZ, 'Poverty assessment study survey: Distribution of poverty in Manicaland Province', Ministry of Public Service, Labour and Social Welfare – Social Development Fund, 1995b, p. 25.

[6]   Ibid., p. 45.

[7]   GOZ, 'Poverty assessment study survey: Distribution of poverty in Mashonaland East Province', Ministry of Public Service, Labour and Social Welfare – Social Development Fund, 1995c, p. 1.

[8]   Ibid., p. 25.

and Harare revealed that dried fruits realized approximately double the price of fresh fruits.[9]

Data upon which this paper is based was collected during visits to the study areas. Four visits were made to Rusitu Valley between November 1999 and August 2000. The first visit in November 1999 was aimed at assessing the activities of the womenfolk. The second visit in January 2000 was to prepare some of the women for training in food processing under the ZIMWESI Project.[10] The third visit was in February and March 2000, when training was conducted. The fourth visit in August 2000 was a follow-up to the training activities.

Murewa Food Processing Association was visited between December 1999 and May 2000. The information was gathered through semi-structured interviews, group discussions and general observation of the women during processing. Observations were used to gain knowledge on the production cycle and how it fitted into the day-to-day household activities. Selection of those to be interviewed depended on availability: those producers who were available at the processing centres were interviewed. The first visit was in December 1999. Ranche House College provided an introduction to the area and its inhabitants. Further visits were carried out to determine the activities of the food processors, the problems being faced and possible solutions to these problems.

---

9   The price per unit weight in the same store averaged nineteen times more for dried fruit. Against this, fruit loses approximately 90 per cent of its weight in the drying process. See E. Manzungu and R. Machiridza, 'A survey of the distribution of and consumer preference for dried fruits and vegetables in the Harare/Chitungwiza metropolis', typescript, 2000.
10   Zimbabwe Programme for Women Studies, Extension, Sociology and Irrigation – a joint programme between the University of Zimbabwe and Wageningen Agricultural University in the Netherlands, which carries out research for the improvement of rural livelihoods and lives.

Overview of the study areas

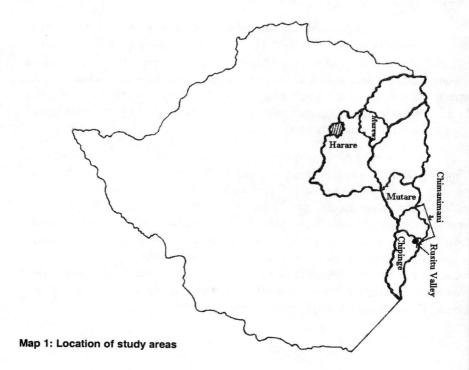

Map 1: Location of study areas

The map shows the location of the two study areas. Rusitu Valley is situated in south-eastern Zimbabwe in Chipinge District. The area is characterized as suitable for intensive agriculture. Temperatures and rainfall are high, resulting in lush vegetation. The Valley is mountainous, however, and there are shops and administrative offices on some of the flat land, leaving very little land for agricultural production. Inhabitants of the Valley have resorted to clearing fields and building their homes on mountainsides. Roads are also constructed on the sides of the mountains making them dangerous, especially during the rainy season when they become muddy and slippery.

Due to the mountainous nature of the Valley and the thick vegetation, livestock rearing is limited. Poultry and goats are reared at homesteads, while cattle are kept at a nearby Agricultural Rural Development Authority (ARDA) dairy scheme. ARDA is a parastatal organization. Its mandate is to undertake commercial farming on government-owned farms and to ensure rural development through assistance in various agricultural projects.

As in most rural communities, agricultural crop production is the mainstay of the Valley. However, unlike most rural communities in the country, very little of the staple maize crop is produced because of the wet conditions. Consequently, inhabitants of the Valley buy maize or maize meal. Winter wheat and tea are also produced, usually by farmers fortunate enough to have irrigation systems. There are, however, plenty of fruits. Bananas are the mainstay of the Valley. Every farmer owns a plot of bananas, which produces all the year round. Other fruits produced include mangoes, avocado pears, oranges, pineapples, tangerines and guavas.

The market for fresh products is limited by the poor state of the roads into the Valley and the very limited demand within it. The marketing dilemma has been exacerbated by the introduction of improved varieties of fruits through the intervention of ARDA and the Agricultural Technical and Extension Services (AGRITEX). These resulted in greater yields when the local market was already limited. Several farmers' associations have been formed, such as the Rusitu Valley Fruit Growers Association and the Rusitu Valley Tea Growers Association. Membership of these is by payment of a joining fee and monthly subscriptions thereafter. Associations collect the produce from the farmers and identify markets. This has reduced the difficulty farmers faced in looking for transport to seek uncertain markets. Some farmers, however, still travel out of the Valley to seek markets for their produce because they are not members of the associations. Some members perceive the associations as robbing them because the associations sell the produce at much higher prices than those paid to the farmers. The farmers allege that the committee members put the difference into their own pockets, while the committee members say that the profits are used for administrative and running expenses (payment of drivers, maintenance of the vehicles and post-harvest treatment of the fruits).

Rusitu Valley Jam Canners' Association, an all-women jam-making association, is another feature of the Valley, and is the focus of this study. The Association has provided a further market for fruits from the Valley.

Murewa, which is rated as of marginal potential for semi-intensive agriculture, is situated about 100 kilometres from the city of Harare, in Mashonaland East Province. Farming activities in the area hinge around the production of the staple maize crop. The area also boasts an abundance of the mango fruit, which made the area a prime candidate in fruit and vegetable drying.

Farmers from Murewa also experience problems in marketing. This is in spite of the fact that the area is very close to Harare and that transport is consequently available. The problem is that farmers do not have money to hire vehicles for transporting fruits to the market.

Hope and politics in Rusitu Valley

The beginning and the process

The Rusitu Valley Jam Canners' Association was formally started in 1982 with a membership of about 115 women. Initially, the women were members of clubs, where they were involved in dressmaking and baking activities. The clubs were amalgamated in the early 1980s, and the Association was born. It was formed with the purpose of ensuring the utilization of fruits that were plentiful and had no readily available market. Members themselves moulded bricks and gathered building materials for their canning factory. They received financial assistance to pay the constructors from the Canadian International Development Agency (CIDA). CIDA also donated a cold-room, freezers and electric boilers.

In December 1999, membership stood at 65 after some of the members withdrew. Death has not greatly affected the membership since daughters and daughters-in-law take the places of the deceased. Some members left because of the workload when the premises of the Association were being built, while others left because they were gainfully employed and could not afford the time. The clubs had permitted gainfully employed women to be members as meetings were held once a week. When the Association was first formed, the women were expected to work at the Association every day. This was not possible for those who had other employment. Some members decided to leave because the proceeds from processing were low and they felt that it was more profitable to work in the fields. A few members pulled out because of old age and ill health, exacerbated by the long distances they had to travel to and from the Association premises. Membership is made up of mostly old women with the majority (75 per cent) above 46 years old. About half of these are above 56 years old.

The members were divided into three working groups. These groups take turns to work at the Association. Each group works a total of two days per week. Members are placed under group leaders, also called quality controllers, who supervize the production process.

Pineapples, mangoes, oranges, guavas produced in the valley and plums bought from neighbouring commercial farms are used for making jam. The Association buys fruits from farmers in the Valley at $1 per kilogramme. At times when the Association is strapped for cash, the members bring fruit from their homes for no payment. The processing procedure is shown in Box 1.

Box 1: Processing procedure

❖ The women select the fruits and weigh them using a fish-scale. The fruits are washed, peeled and cut up (if necessary).

❖ Fruits are boiled and sieved (using mutton cloth) to extract the juice.

❖ The juice is boiled with sugar until the mixture is thick.

❖ This is emptied out of the boiler into plastic buckets where the colourant is added.

❖ Cans are lined up and manually filled using cups.

❖ After filling, lids are placed on the cans and these are sealed (mechanically or manually).

❖ The sealed cans are cooled in a bucket of cold water after which they are labelled (using ordinary glue) and put in the storeroom.

NB: *In between the boiling, sieving and addition of sugar, the fruits and juice are kept in the cold-room and/or freezers.*

The Association produces pure fruit jams, mixed fruit jam and marmalade. The mixed fruit jam is produced from all the fruits except citrus fruits, which are used for the marmalade. Pure fruit jams can be produced from all the fruits. Pineapple jam is the most popular with customers. Production is, however, limited because of the peeling process, which is time-consuming, and the fact that pineapples give very little juice per unit weight of fresh fruit. This gives less cans of jam compared to other fruits. Consequently the Association produces more marmalade and mixed fruit jam.

Markets and technology

The jam is sold to boarding schools in the Chipinge and Chimanimani Districts. These schools (Rusitu, Biriwiri and Chibuwe mission schools) are supplied with jam every school term. The Association also sells its jam to community members although this does not bring in much money (approximately $1,000[11] per month). A few members travel out of the Valley and sell the jam, but this does not bring in much money.

The women say that making jam clashes with their household and farming activities. The clash is most felt during the rainy season when the women need to work in their fields while the soils are still moist. The women sometimes employ casual labour in their fields while they work at the Association.

Another problem relates to the production process. The processing procedure, as indicated in Box 1, is manual (with the exception of the electric can sealer) since the Association does not have equipment for machine processing. Manual processing is slow and involves a heavy workload, which is strenuous for elderly members.

The equipment used also presents problems. One example is the knives. These are sharpened in the traditional method by rubbing the blade on a stone. As the knives do not keep their edge for long, the work is tiresome and slow. The boilers at the Association are also said to be slow in heating up and of low capacity. During one of the visits to the Association, one of the boilers was no longer functioning. This, according to the women, resulted in heavy losses especially during the peak production season when some fruits had to be thrown away because the remaining boiler could not hold them all. The can-sealer was reported to be giving the women problems, as they had to change stands for the different sizes of cans (450g and 900g). The sealer breaks down frequently and the women have to pay a mechanic for repairs. When the sealer is not working, the cans are sealed using a manually operated can-sealer. Productivity is reduced because the women find the manual sealer heavy and difficult to operate. The Association had to send one of its members for training on how to repair the electric sealer. However, the age and illiteracy of the trainee presented problems: she forgot what she had been taught and a mechanic still had to be paid. The process of filling the cans, sealing, cooling and labelling them is also time-consuming. The women said that they would have liked to have a conveyor belt to assist them.

Some members of the Association said that they needed more markets for their produce while others disagreed. The members who said they did not need more markets argued that they were failing to supply the current markets and

---

11   At that time, approximately US$30.

could therefore not handle more. Those members who said they needed more markets said that they could supply more markets if only they were not limited by the technology at the Association.

Boarding schools in the district represented a reliable market for their products. However, there were problems here too. Some of the schools asked the Association to use 2kg cans instead of the 450g and 900g cans currently in use, saying this would curb thefts of the product by workers at the schools. The Association cannot supply these because the can-sealer in use does not have a 2kg stand and the Association does not have the money to buy the required equipment. The major problem seems to be that the target market was not defined when production was started, especially for bulk buyers such as schools.

The Association also approached the retail supermarkets, OK and TM, and wholesalers Bhadella and Jaggers. The Association could not meet their packaging requirements: the supermarkets wanted the jam to be bottled, not canned, and the Association was unable to meet the stringent sterilization requirements of bottling. During the early days of the Association, jam was bottled but had a reduced shelf life as it developed mould. Without adequate equipment for sterilization, the women switched to canning the jam. The wholesalers wanted the canned products in transparent plastic cartons of six or twelve cans each. The Association did not have the financial resources to purchase the required packaging materials. Another limitation was that the Association did not have a stamp of approval from the Standards Association of Zimbabwe.

Finance and politics

The Association uses the proceeds from the sale of jam for operation and management costs. Expenses at the Association include the paying of salaries: $8,320 (US$146.22) goes to salaries and wages every month. The Association pays 65 members, each working sixteen hours a week, at a rate of $2 per hour. Each member receives at most $128 per month. This amounts to $1,536 per year. According to the 1995 Poverty Assessment Study Survey,[12] such payments are sufficient only to feed one person without addressing the education, clothing and

---

[12] The calculated FPL and TCPL are most likely to have increased considerably in view of the current economic status of the country, implying that the incomes are below the FPL, thus qualifying these women as very poor. Consultations revealed that no new values had been calculated since the 1995 survey.

health needs of the individual. The women themselves said that they could not send their children to school on the payments they received from the Association. They only manage to buy a bar of soap and a packet of sugar. Some months the women do not receive their wages because the money is channelled to the purchase of raw materials or running costs.

Additional money is paid to the committee members because they have to be at the Association's premises every day. They are paid for 40 hours of work per week, and earn a total of $640 per month. This is five times more than the other members. These women receive a total of $7,680 per year. The ordinary members say that the leaders of the different working groups could do the committee members' work. The committee members, however, say that they cannot delegate their work to group leaders because it would create discrepancies in the record books. They say that they have to get paid more as compensation for the hours they spend at the Association, hours they could have been working in their fields.

The chairperson is also paid for 40 hours in a week. Complaints have been levelled against this lady, who is accused of misusing Association funds. According to the members, and personal observation, the chairperson is hardly at the Association, travelling around supposedly to source potential markets to increase cash income. The chairperson, who owns a grocery store in the Valley, is accused of travelling round on personal business and getting her expenses met by the Association.

The Association also pays a driver to use the pick-up truck to transport jam to the boarding schools during the school term. A security guard is paid to look after the premises at night. An insurance premium of $1,000 is paid every four months. Electricity costs around $3,000 per month during the peak processing period. Raw materials such as fruits, labels, cans, sugar, glue and colourant are also purchased from time to time. Detailed records of accounts at the Association were not available. Ordinary members of the Association could not give any information on the accounts and referred all questions to the chairperson, who was hardly at the Association.

Generally, the members feel that their lives have not benefited much from the Association. They say that they have nothing tangible to show for their eighteen years spent with the Association. Their pride will not let them leave because of the ridicule they suffered from other community members who predicted failure from the beginning. The ordinary members hope to get the Association's assets sold so that they can share the proceeds. This could take some time because the chairperson is said to have verbally assaulted the women when she heard of these plans. The members say that the chairperson does not want the Association sold because she is surviving off it.

However, some of the members, said that they had benefited from the Association. These members, it emerged, were related to committee members. In spite of these problems, activities at the Association continue with ordinary members biding their time.

Diversification

The Association is planning more projects to boost cash income, such as fruit and vegetable drying. The Association was assisted by the ZIMWESI project in November 1999. At the time the Association was visited, there were plans to visit Ranche House College, an adult education institute in Harare, for training in fruit and vegetable drying. The ZIMWESI project offered to pay the full costs of the exercise, which was in February 2000. A follow-up visit in August 2000 revealed that the women were only drying vegetables for their own consumption and for sale to other community members. The Association cited inadequate financial resources as the crippling factor, explaining that they could not purchase the equipment required for processing. However, the chairperson said that the Association had set aside about $3,000 as start-up capital for fruit and vegetable drying.

The Association has a small plot where during the rainy season members produce maize for sale, either fresh or dry. During the dry season, they grow vegetables for sale.

The Association also plans to engage in dressmaking and has already purchased sewing machines. Finance is limiting the purchase of fabrics to sew. Other planned activities include processing peanut butter, extracting fruit juice, pressing oil, milling grain and baking bread.

Technology blues in Murewa

Introducing fruit and vegetable drying

Ranche House College introduced the drying of fruit and vegetables in Murewa in 1995. One hundred and twenty participants were trained in the technical aspects of fruit and vegetable drying and in the management of the business, including keeping records. Only about ten per cent of the original trainees remain, with the existing groups being made up of new trainees of Ranche House College. The first graduates of Ranche House College in the area also trained people to assist them in fruit and vegetable drying. The College trained the women in Murewa to work as individuals who would be accomplished entrepreneurs in their own right and thereby improve their social status. Trainees however preferred to work as groups instead of as individuals. Those who initiated the project had focused on women only, but the women felt that having males as part of the exercise would make it easier for them to have access to resources, and introduced some men into their teams.

Processing activities

When the area was first visited in December 1999, there were seven processing groups at three processing sites, namely Nyamutumbu, Ngwerume and Forty-four Miles business centres. The groups involved in processing were Ngwerume A, Ngwerume B, Nyamutumbu Team 1, Nyamutumbu Team 2, Nyamutumbu Chitsiku Unit, Forty-four Miles Six Star Unit and Forty-four Miles Nyamuzara Unit. When we visited the area in January 2000, the three groups in Nyamutumbu had merged. After the merger, the groups that were actively involved in processing were Ngwerume A and B and the Nyamutumbu team.

Most of the processors were female subsistence farmers. They were also involved in other activities such as looking after their families, farming, rearing livestock and social obligations such as funerals. These activities were given preference over food processing, resulting in limited time being spent at the processing sites. The work at home was increased by the fact that some of the men in the area worked in the city, leaving the women as the effective household heads. One of the women in the Nyamutumbu group operated a grocery store on a full-time basis, while a member of the Forty-four Miles Six Star unit owned a hair salon. Another female member of the Forty-four Miles Nyamuzara Unit was involved in marketing dairy products and market gardening. Some of the members considered processing to be a part-time activity. As a consequence, processing activities suffered. Members met at most three days a week to undertake processing.

The process of drying fruits is presented in the box opposite.

Box 2: Preparation of mangoes for drying

Processing hygiene

❖ Processors wash their hands and arms with fresh water followed by bleach solution (200cc JIK to ten litres of clean water), which destroys microbes that would contaminate the fruits, before processing. Afterwards they wear clean intact plastic gloves, aprons and cover their heads.

Individual selection

❖ The working area and utensils should be cleaned first with fresh water and then with bleach solution.

❖ Fruits are selected individually removing under- and over-ripe, rotten and/or damaged fruits.

❖ Fruits are weighed.

Individual washing

❖ Fruits are individually washed in fresh water after which they are carefully washed in dilute bleach solution ensuring that the skin is not broken.

Peeling and slicing

❖ Clean, sharp, stainless steel knives should be used for peeling, ensuring minimal removal of flesh.

❖ Fruits should be sliced to uniform thickness (approximately 3 mm). Slices thicker than this would take longer to dry while thinner slices tend to be brittle. Uniformity also adds appeal.

❖ Trays for loading the fruits are cleaned using fresh water and bleach solution.

❖ Fruits are loaded onto trays as they are sliced to facilitate drying.

❖ Trays are loaded into the dryers one at a time when they are full.

❖ The dryer has to be tightly shut to keep out dust and insects.

❖ Mangoes are left in the dryer until the following day when they are turned over. They are removed from the dryer on the next day. Appropriate moisture content is determined by wrapping a slice around the finger without the slice sticking to the hand or breaking.

❖ The slices are removed from the trays into plastic buckets to be weighed and packaged later.

The solar dryer is made up of transparent plastic covering a wooden frame (2.2 metres by 1.6 metres) and raised 0.6 metres above the ground. The dryer has two shelves each holding three trays (1.5 metres by 0.6 metres each) on which the fresh products are laid out to dry. The door to the dryer should be fixed tightly to keep out insects and dust. It is advised that the dryer be placed on concrete slabs to reduce contamination of the products by dust.

The practices of the groups differed. The Nyamutumbu group was the only one in which members followed all the technical regulations according to the training procedure, for example wearing their processing gear comprising aprons, hats and gloves. The working area was well-tended with the dryers in good sanitary condition. The males in the groups refused to clean the working area and processing utensils, alleging that this was women's work.

Members of Ngwerume A group sometimes wore processing gear. Some of the members were not aware of the need for keeping records. There were however rudimentary records of financial transactions available. Members did not practise stringent hygiene as they piled trays one on top of the other when taking them to the dryer. The appropriate practice is to carry one tray at a time, which ensures that microbial transfer is limited. The dryers were infested with flies and the surroundings overgrown with grass. To add to this, there was a pool of stagnant water by the dryers. These factors contribute to the poor quality of produce from the processors.

Record keeping

Trainees had to keep records of raw materials and processing data focusing on the weight processed and harvested, weight of debris, weather conditions at time of processing, time of loading and unloading the dryer. Financial transactions, such as costs of raw materials and cash brought in from the sale of dried products, had to be recorded.

It was clear that the trainees did not understand the importance of keeping records. Information contained in the records was disjointed. Nyamutumbu was the only group that had informative records stretching back to 1998, which included the original plans of the group. The group planned to dry mangoes and store them for sale when the mango season was over in order to avoid competition with the fresh products. During the 1999 season, they planned to process about 65 tonnes of fresh mangoes to produce about 6.5 tonnes of dry product. Processors hoped to make a net profit of about $2,000,000 that year, selling a 50g packet of dried mangoes for $20.

The records however showed that production levels were in fact very low with the group realizing an income of only $9,450 in the season. Plans were based on a drying cycle of a harvest of 30 kilogrammes of produce per cycle repeated three times a week using 35 dryers. This did not materialize because of the limitation in dryers, raw materials and because processors did not always turn up for processing on the assigned days. Some members turned up late for processing resulting in the processing exercise starting late in the day. This reduced the time products were exposed to the sun, thus reducing the ultimate harvest.

The records also revealed that ten per cent of the mangoes ended up as waste, because they were over-ripe, under-ripe, damaged or spoilt. Of the 90 per cent that were accepted, 40 per cent formed the debris (peels and seeds).

Constraints of fruit and vegetable drying

Constraints faced by different groups were similar, differing only in extent between the different groups. The constraints were related to raw materials, technology, markets and finance.

Availability of raw materials in the area is limited. Fruits in Murewa ripen in February when the rainy season is at its peak. Drying mangoes during this time is a problem because there is very little sunshine, and mangoes have to spend longer than two days in the dryer. These products are said to taste as if they have been fermented, as revealed by a study we carried out in Harare and Chitungwiza on customer preference. To boost production, mangoes are bought from Mutoko and the Eastern Highlands or other areas which have mangoes that ripen early. The processors however indicated that they had problems with this arrangement because they did not have transport to ferry the raw materials from these areas to their processing sites. Consequently, they could not make firm arrangements with the farmers when the latter could not supply them with fruit immediately. Some processors travelled to Harare to buy mangoes that would have been transported from Mutoko. This has contributed to the low turnover of the groups.

The solar dryer, although supposed to be easily operated by rural inhabitants, has presented some problems. It requires constant replacement of timber during the rainy season and plastic when it is hot. Processors complain that they do not have the money to buy these materials. The dryer also presents problems during the rainy season because of limited sunshine, which results in reduced product harvests. Conditions in the dryer are not controlled, resulting in mangoes sometimes being over-dried or under-dried. Under-dried products tend to spoil easily while over-dried products are said to be papery and to lose their flavour. The limitation in technology also results in mangoes being harvested from the fields when they are under-ripe to ensure continued production. Waiting for the fruits to ripen would result in very little production, because by the time they ripen the rainy season will be at its peak. Some of the processors have decided to buy electric dryers to assist or replace the solar dryers. However, electric dryers are expensive and the processors hope that they will obtain donations to help them purchase the equipment. The processors also say that the solar dryers are of low capacity and that this limits the harvest. However, an increase in size would result in a reduction of the heat circulating in the dryer. This would increase the time taken by one drying cycle.

Some of the new graduates of Ranche House College had to borrow dryers from some of the first graduates because they did not have their own. This crippled processing activities because the old groups then denied the new groups the use of their dryers. The new graduates had to hold up their processing until dryers were available.

The groups market their produce under the name Murewa Food Processors Association. Initially, the groups sold their produce to Wholesale Fruiterers, who in turn distributed it to other retailers. Wholesale Fruiterers asked the processors to supply them with 500 packets of dried fruit per week. The quality of the produce was not specified. The processors unfortunately failed to supply the required quantities so they lost the market. They said that they had problems sourcing raw materials in sufficient quantities. The technology also made it difficult for them to harvest large quantities because mangoes take about two days to dry, resulting in mangoes being harvested only twice a week. On average the more committed processors produced about 31 packets of mangoes per cycle resulting in about 62 packets of mangoes per week. For the seven groups this added up to only 434 packets a week. Our observations suggested that the greatest problem was that the processors treated fruit and vegetable drying as a part-time activity for times when they were not busy with other activities.

The processors also approached companies such as Lever Brothers, Lemco and other producers of texturized proteins and soups. The companies gave the processors specifications on texture, moisture and microbial contents in the products. Lever Brothers asked that the products be dried under controlled conditions in incubators. Financial limitations meant that the processors could not buy the required equipment to supply these markets. Ranche House College made reference to a foreign market for dried fruits in the Netherlands, which required about a tonne of dried produce per year. The total produced by all groups averaged only around 120 kilogrammes in a season.

The groups complained about inadequate financial resources. They had been receiving financial assistance for processing activities from several sources, including the Agricultural Finance Corporation (AFC). The money was for the building of processing premises and did not extend to the purchase of raw materials and day-to-day operations. The money was however embezzled by an employee of Ranche House College, who had been tasked to assist the women.

Building materials donated to the processors were allegedly misused by some of the members. One female member, who owns a hair salon, was said to have used the materials to construct boarding rooms at her premises. Some of the materials were used as payment for the builders of the processing premises because of a shortage of cash. Processors say that they do not have money to buy labels and packaging materials and to transport raw materials for processing. Inadequate finances are also blamed for the failure to acquire more and better technology to improve production.

Discussion and conclusions

We have shown that the efforts to alleviate poverty through small-scale food processing by outside agents were on the whole not successful. This is not simply because the women failed to grasp the technical aspects of small-scale food processing. Rather it had to do with women's social setting, which was poorly understood. Related to this, the organizational requirements for the new technologies were very much under-estimated. The technology of small-scale food processing needs to be embedded within the social, economic and cultural milieu of the women.

Our evidence shows that small-scale food processing in Rusitu Valley and Murewa District failed to improve the livelihoods of the women participants. Indeed, it can be argued that the women were worse off after they embarked on processing.

In both cases, women ended up with more work but with little benefit accruing to them. In Rusitu Valley, the women earned only $128 per month after committing considerable resources in time and fruits to the Association. This failure to secure a better life for the rural women needs to be explained so that the same mistakes can be avoided in future.

In the first instance, we observe that small-scale food processing as it was practised was not an idea that arose from within the community, but was conceived of by outsiders. As a consequence, there were gaps in knowledge, which resulted in the failure of the exercise. For example, there was no consideration of the fact that the intended time for drying mangoes in Murewa coincided with the peak rainy season in the area. There was no plan for times when there was no sunshine. This compromised the impacts of food processing. Some of the trainees abandoned the exercise or committed very little time to it.

At the heart of the problem is the lack of understanding of the social shaping of technology. The outside planners viewed technology as a tool that can easily be deployed to solve all problems. Technology development and design are in fact social processes in which different stakeholders interact. The nature of the process and the different perceptions and interests of the stakeholders shape the characteristics of the technologies. The trainers were also not aware of the social relations of the people they were trying to help. The disadvantaged status of women limits their access to resources.

The College offered training to the women in Murewa with the intention that the trainees would work as individuals. The capacity of the solar dryers was too low for the number of people trying to use them. The solar technology advocated by the trainers proved to be unreliable and in constant need of repair. In the Rusitu case, the manual can-sealer was too heavy for the old women to operate. The electric can-sealer on the other hand presented problems in that the women could not repair it.

Technology also has social impacts on users. One common impact was the competition for time that ensues between the new and existing activities. The Murewa food processors committed more time to farming activities than to food processing. Two arguments could explain this. The first is that the women probably saw more potential in existing activities. Another possible explanation could be that the processors in the area had not invested much in the new exercise. The solar dryers could hardly be called big investments. Because of this, the women could afford to shelve processing. In Rusitu Valley, on the other hand, the women had buildings, a cold room, freezers and electric boilers. The women could therefore not afford to abandon processing. The Association in Rusitu Valley has become a sort of bondage to the women: although they might want to leave, they cannot easily do so.

The case studies showed problems that might have been partly avoided if the intended recipients of the intervention had been allowed greater participation in its planning. Such participation would have brought to light the social structures in the area, revealing potential limitations. Intended recipients would also have been shown what was required of them and what the impacts of the intervention would be. They would have had the opportunity to choose to take up the project, adjust it, or reject it. In short, technology is as much social as it is technical.

Another point is the inadequacy of financial resources. The interventions aimed to increase the cash available to the women and thus improve their lives. The interventions did not however address the fact that the women did not have the financial resources for access to better technology and raw materials. Many interventions have fallen by the wayside because the intended beneficiaries did not have the funds to sustain the project. There is therefore still need for money-lending institutions that take cognizance of the circumstances of the recipients.

Contributors

Paradzai Bongo was a student researcher and teaching assistant in the Department of Sociology, University of Zimbabwe.

Dr Michael Bourdillon is Professor in Social Anthropology in the Department of Sociology, the University of Zimbabwe. His most recent work has been on working children, out of which came the edited volume, Earning a Life: Working Children in Zimbabwe, Weaver Press, Harare, 2000.

Stephen Buzuzi was a post-graduate student in the Department of Sociology, University of Zimbabwe.

Dr Paul Hebinck teaches in Department of Social Sciences – Rural Development Sociology, Wageningen University, The Netherlands. He has worked for about twenty years in Africa, mostly on social processes in agricultural and rural development.

Rose Machiridzi was a post-graduate research assistant from the Department of Agricultural Economics and Extension, University of Zimbabwe. She is now pursuing her post-graduate studies at the University of Wageningen.

Dr Ismael Magaisa is a lecturer in the Department of Sociology, University of Zimbabwe. His doctoral research on prostitutes in Harare has been accepted by University of Zimbabwe Publications.

Stanford Mahati was a post-graduate student researcher in the Department of Sociology, University of Zimbabwe.

Jaqueline Mangoma was a post-graduate student and teaching assistant in the Department of Sociology, University of Zimbabwe. She is now a medical research officer at the Blair Research Institute in Harare.

Dr Emmanuel Manzungu was the co-ordinator of the ZIMWESI project on the Zimbabwean side from 1998-2000, and edited a book on irrigation arising out of the project. Currently he is a research associate in the Department of Soil Science and Agricultural Engineering at the University of Zimbabwe.

Rekopantswe Mate is a lecturer in the Department of Sociology, University of Zimbabwe. Her interests include gender and the family.

Consolidated Bibliography

Agarwal, B., 'Gender, property and rights: Bridging a critical gap in economic analysis and policy', in E. Kuiper, J. Sap *et al.*, (eds), *Out of the margin: Feminist perspectives on economics*, Routledge, London, 1995.

Aldridge, J. and S. Becker, *Children who care: Inside the world of young carers*, Department of Social Sciences, Loughborough University, 1993.

Argent, J. and T. O'Riordan, 'The North Sea', in J. X. Karperson *et al.*, *Regions at Risk: Comparisons of Threatened Environments*, United Nations University Press, New York, 1995, pp. 367-419.

Attfield, R., *The Ethics of Environmental Concern*, Basil Blackwell, Oxford, 1983.

Bass, C. and S. Sargent, 'The future shape of forests', in Johan Holmberg (ed.), *Policies for a Small Planet*, 2nd edn, Earthscan Publications, London, 1992.

Bassey, M. W. and O. G. Schmidt, *Abrasive-disk Dehullers in Africa: From Research to Dissemination*, IDRC, Ottawa, 1989.

Bennett, T. W., *Human Rights and African Customary Law*, Juta and Co., Cape Town, 1995.

Berlyn, P., 'Some aspects of the material culture of the Shona people', *NADA*, Vol. 9, No. 5, 1968.

Bongo, P. and M. F. C. Bourdillon, 'Intervention in natural resource use in Biriwiri'. *Zambezia*, Vol. 28, No. 2, 2001, pp. 133-46.

Bourdieu, P., *Outline of a Theory of Practice*, Cambridge University Press, 1977.

Bourdillon, M. F. C. and M. Mutisi, 'Child vendors at a rural growth point', in M. F. C. Bourdillon (ed.), *Earning a Life: Working Children in Zimbabwe*, Harare, Weaver Press, 2000, pp. 75-94.

Bourdillon, M. F. C., 'Children at work on tea and coffee estates', in M. F. C. Bourdillon (ed.), *Earning a Life: Working Children in Zimbabwe*, Weaver Press, Harare, 2000, pp. 147-172.

Bourdillon, M. F. C., 'Child labour and education: A case study from south-eastern Zimbabwe', *Journal of Social Development in Africa*, Vol. 15, No. 2, 2000, pp. 5-32.

Boyden, Jocelyn, '*The relationship between education and child work*', Innocenti Occasional Papers, No. 9, UNICEF, 1994.

Bromley, K. A., R. C. Hannington, G. B. Jones and C. J. Lightfoot, 'Melsetter Regional plan', Department of Conservation and Extension, Harare, 1968.

Brown, D., 'Participatory biodiversity conservation: Rethinking the strategy in low tourist potential areas of tropical Africa', Overseas Development Institute, No. 33, August 1998.

Campbell, B. *et al.*, 'Tree and woodland resources: The technical practices of small-scale farmers', in P. N. Bradley and K. McNamara (eds) 'Living with trees: Policies for forest management in Zimbabwe', World Bank Technical Paper, No. 210, Washington D. C., The World Bank, 1993, pp. 29-62.

Carney, D. (ed.), 'Sustainable rural livelihoods: What contributions can we make?', DFID, London, 1998.

Carney, D., 'Social capital. Key sheets for sustainable livelihoods: Policy, planning and implementation', Department for International Development, ODI, London, 1999.

Chambers, R., *Whose Reality Counts? Putting the First Last*, Intermediate Technology Publications, London, 1997.

Cheal, D., 'Strategies of resource management in household economics: Moral economy or political economy?', in R. McC. Netting, R. Wilk and E. Arnould, *The Household Economy: Reconsidering the Domestic Mode of Production*, Westview Press, Boulder (Colorado), 1989.

Cheater, A. P., 'Anthropologists and policy in Zimbabwe: Design at the centre, and reactions on the periphery', in R. Grillo and A. Rew (eds), *Social Anthropology and Development Policy*, Tavistock Publications, London and New York, 1985, pp. 58-72.

Cheater, A. P., *Idioms of Accumulation*, Mambo Press, Gweru, 1986.

Chigumira, P., 'The potential for extruded sorghum food products in Zimbabwe and the regional market', in M. I. Gomez *et al.*, *'Utilization of Sorghum and Millets'*, ICRISAT, Andhra Pradesh, 1992, pp. 89-94.

Chinsman, B., 'Choice of technique in sorghum and millet hulling in Africa', proceedings of ICC 11 Congress, Vienna, Austria, 1984.

Chirwa, Y. and M. F. C. Bourdillon, 'Small-scale commercial farming: Working children in Nyanyadzi irrigation scheme', in M. F. C. Bourdillon (ed.), *Earning a Life: Working Children in Zimbabwe*, Weaver Press, Harare, 2000, pp. 127-145.

Contrucci, J. and A. Collard, *Rape of the Wild: Man's Violence Against Animals and the Earth*, The Women's Press, London, 1988.

Cotsgrove, S., 'Environmentalism and Utopia', *Sociological Review*, Vol. 24, 1976, pp. 23-42.

Crehan, K. and A. van Oppen, 'Understanding of "development": An arena of struggle. The story of a development project in Zambia', *Sociologia Ruralis*, Vol. 28, No. 2/3, 1988, pp. 113-146.

Davies, H. R., Jr, 'Agriculture, food and the colonial period', in A. Hansen and D. E. McMillan (eds), *Food in Sub-Saharan Africa*, Lynne Rienner Publishers, Colorado, 1986, pp. 151-168.

Davis, W., 'The Land Must Live', in K. S. Shrader-Frechette (ed.), *Environmental Ethics*, Boxwood Press, California, 1981.

De Sardan, J. P., 'Peasant logics and the development project logics', *Sociologia Ruralis*, Vol. 28, No. 2/3, 1988, pp. 216-226.

Einarsson, N., 'All animals are equal but some are cetaceans: Conservation and culture conflict', in K. Milton (ed.), *Environmentalism: The View from Anthropology*, Routledge, 1993, pp. 73-84.

Ellert, H., *The Material Culture of Zimbabwe*, Harare, Longman, 1984.

Ellis, F., *Rural Livelihoods and Diversity in Developing Countries*, Oxford University Press, 2000.

FAO, 'Processing and storage of foodgrains by rural families', *Agricultural Services Bulletin*, No. 53, Rome, 1983.

FAO, 'Post-harvest and processing technologies for African staple foods: A technical compendium', *Agricultural Services Bulletin*, No. 89, Rome, 1991.

FAO and ICRISAT, 'The world sorghum and millet economics: Facts, trends and outlook', a joint study by the Basic Foodstuffs Service, FAO Commodities and Trade Division and the Socio-economics and Policy Division, International Crops Research Institute for the Semi-Arid Tropics (ICRISAT), India and Rome, 1996.

Fapohunda, E., 'The non-pooling household: A challenge to the theory', in D. Dwyer and J. Bruce (eds), *A Home Divided: Women and Income in the Third World*, Stanford University Press, Stanford, 1988.

Fellows, P. (ed.), *Traditional Foods: Processing for Profit*, Intermediate Technology Publications, London, 1997.

Forestry Commission, 'Woodland and tree management programme for dry areas in Zimbabwe', unpublished paper prepared for Overseas Development Agency, 1995.

Fortmann, L. and C. Nhira, 'Local management of trees and woodland resources in Zimbabwe: A tenurial niche approach', Centre for Applied Social Sciences, University of Zimbabwe, Harare, 1992.

Francis, E., *Making a Living, Changing Livelihoods in Rural Africa*, Routledge, London, 2000.

Frank, E., *Peasant Economics: Farm Households and Agrarian Development*, 2nd edn, Cambridge University Press, 1993.

Gaidzanwa, R. B., 'Land, the economic empowerment of women: A gendered analysis', *Southern African Feminist Review*, Vol. 1, No. 1, 1995, pp. 1-12.

Gelfand, M., *Growing Up in Shona Society: From Birth to Marriage*, Mambo Press, Gweru, 1979.

Giroux, H. A., 'Resisting difference: Cultural studies and the discourse of critical pedagogy', in L. Grossberg *et al.*, *Cultural Studies*, London and New York, Routledge, 1992.

Godelier, M., *The Mental and the Material*, Verso, London and New York, 1980.

Gomez, M. I. *et al.*, 'Utilization of Sorghum and Millets', ICRISAT, Andhra Pradesh, 1992.

Government of Zimbabwe, 'Poverty assessment study survey: Distribution of poverty in Zimbabwe', Ministry of Public Service, Labour and Social Welfare – Social Development Fund, 1995.

Government of Zimbabwe, 'Poverty assessment study survey: Distribution of poverty in Manicaland Province', Ministry of Public Service, Labour and Social Welfare – Social Development Fund, 1995.

Government of Zimbabwe, 'Poverty assessment study survey: Distribution of poverty in Mashonaland East Province', Ministry of Public Service, Labour and Social Welfare – Social Development Fund, 1995.

Government of Zimbabwe, 'Zimbabwe 1999 National Child Labour Survey', Central Statistical Office, Harare, 1999.

Guyer, J., 'Household and community in African studies', *African Studies Review*, Vol. 24, No. 2/3, 1981, pp. 87-138.

Hatton, J. C., 'Status quo assessment of the Chimanimani Transfrontier Conservation Area', a report to Departmento National de Floresta e Fauna Bravia, Maputo, 1995.

Hedden-Dunkhorst, B., 'The contribution of sorghum and millet versus maize to food security in semi-arid Zimbabwe', unpublished D.Phil. thesis, University of Hohenheim, 1993.

Hiebsch, C. and K. S. O'Hair, 'Major domesticated food crops', in A. Hansen and D. E. McMillan (eds), *Food in Sub-Saharan Africa*, Lynne Rienner Publishers, Colorado, 1986, pp. 177-205.

Jacobs, S., 'The gendered politics of land reforms: Three comparative studies', in V. Randall and G. Waylen (eds), *Gender Politics and the State*, Routledge, London, 1998.

Jacobs, S., 'Zimbabwe, state, class and gendered models of land resettlement', in K. L. Staudt and J. L. Parpart (eds), *Patriarchy and Class: African Women in the Home and the Workplace*, Westview Press, Boulder (Colorado), 1989.

James, A., et al., *Theorising Childhood*, Polity Press, Cambridge, 1998.

Jones, S., *Assaulting Childhood: Children's Experiences of Migrancy and Hostel Life in South Africa*, Witwatersrand University Press, Johannesburg, 1993.

Leach, M., R. Mearns and I. Scoones, 'Environmental entitlements: A framework for understanding the institutional dynamics of environmental change', discussion paper No. 359, Institute of Development Studies, University of Sussex, 1996.

Lipton, M., M. de Klerk and M. Lipton (eds), *Land, Labour and Rural Livelihoods in South Africa*, Indicator Press, Durban, 1996.

Littlehood, R., 'Military rape', *Anthropology Today*, Vol. 13, No. 2, 1997, pp. 1-16.

Long, N., *An Introduction to the Sociology of Development*, Tavistock Publications, London, 1997.

Long, N., *Development Sociology: Actor Perspectives*, Routledge, London, 2001.

Long. N. and J. D. van der Ploeg, 'Demythologising planned intervention: An actor perspective', *Sociologia Ruralis*, Vol. 29, No. 3/4, 1989, pp. 226-250.

Long, N. and J. D. van der Ploeg, 'Heterogeneity, actor and structure: Towards a reconstitution of the concept structure', in D. Booth (ed.), *Rethinking Social Development: Theory, Research and Practice*, Longman, London, 1994.

Low, N. and B. Gleeson, *Justice, Society and Nature: An Exploration of Political Ecology*, Routledge, London and New York, 1998.

Lowe, P., J. Murdoch and N. Ward, 'Networks in rural development. Beyond exogenous and endogenous models', in J. D. van der Ploeg and G. van Dijk (eds), *Beyond Modernisation. The Impact of Endogenous Development*, Van Grocum, Assen, 1995, pp. 87-107.

Mackenzie, F., 'Land and territory: The interface between two systems of land tenure, Murang'a District, Kenya', *Africa*, Vol. 59, No. 1, 1989, pp. 91-109.

Madovi, P. B., *Food Handling in Shona Villages of Zimbabwe*, Gordon and Breach Science Publishers, United Kingdom, 1981.

Manzungu, E. and R. Machiridza, 'A survey of the distribution of and consumer preference for dried fruits and vegetables in the Harare/Chitungwiza metropolis', typescript, 2000.

Manzungu, E., M. Machingambi and R. Machiridza, 'An evaluation of small-scale fruit and vegetable drying in Murewa', report prepared for Ranche House College, 2000.

Mazvimavi, K., 'Economic analysis of the competitive position of sorghum and millet in semi-arid, smallholder farming regions of Zimbabwe', unpublished M.Phil. thesis, University of Zimbabwe, 1996.

McKechnie, J. and S. Hobbs, 'Working children: Reconsidering the debates', a report of the International Working Group on Child Labour, Defence for Children International, and the International Society for the Prevention of Child Abuse and Neglect, 1998.

Milton, K. (ed.), *Environmentalism: The View from Anthropology*, Routledge, London and New York, 1995.

Milton, K., *Environmentalism and Cultural Theory: Exploring the Role of Anthropology in Environmental Discourse*, Routledge, London, 1996.

Mlambo, A. S. and E. S. Pangeti, *The Political Economy of the Sugar Industry*, University of Zimbabwe Publications, Harare, 1996.

Mongbo, R., 'The appropriation and dismembering of development intervention. Policy, discourse and practice in the field of rural development in Benin', Ph.D. thesis, Wageningen University, 1995.

Moyo, S., 'A gendered perspective of the land question', *Southern African Feminist Review*, Vol. 1, No. 1, 1995b, pp. 13-31.

Moyo, S., 'The political economy of land acquisition and redistribution in Zimbabwe 1990-1999', *Journal of Southern African Studies*, Vol. 26, No. 1, 2000, pp. 5-28.

Moyo, S., B. Rutherford and D. Amanor-Wilks, 'Land reform and changing social relations for farm workers in Zimbabwe', *Review of African Political Economy*, No. 84, 2000, pp. 180-202.

Moyo, S., *The Land Question*, Sapes Trust, Harare, 1995a.

Muchena, O., 'The changing perceptions of women in agriculture', in M. Rukuni and C. K. Eicher (eds), *Zimbabwe's Agricultural Revolution*, University of Zimbabwe Publications, Harare, 1994.

Muchena, O. N. and E. Vanek, 'From ecology through economics to ethnoscience: Changing perceptions of natural resource management', in D. M. Warren, L. J. Slikkerveer and D. Brokensha (ed.), *The Cultural Dimension of Development: Indigenous Knowledge Systems*, Intermediate Technology Publications, London, 1995, pp. 505-511.

Murombedzi, J. C., 'Need for appropriate local level common property resource management institutions in communal tenure regimes', Centre for Applied Social Sciences, University of Zimbabwe, Harare, 1990.

Murray, C., 'Changing livelihoods in Qwaqwa: Research questions and methods of study', in 'Multiple livelihoods and social change', working paper No. 1, Institute for Development Policy and Management, Manchester University, 1998.

Mutowo, K. M., 'Nyanyadzi Irrigation Scheme: Origin and Development (1936-1965)', B. A. dissertation, Department of Economic History, University of Zimbabwe, 1987.

Muzvidziwa, V., 'Rural-urban linkages: Masvingo's double-rooted female heads of household', *Zambezia*, Vol. 24, No. 2, 1997, pp. 97-123.

Ncube, W., *Family Law in Zimbabwe*, Legal Resources Foundation, Harare, 1989.

Nhira, C., *et al.*, 'Communities as institutions for resource management', Centre for Applied Social Sciences, University of Zimbabwe, Harare, 1998.

Nieuwenhuys, O., *Children's Lifeworlds: Gender, Welfare and Labour in the Developing World*, Routledge, London, 1994.

Oboler, R. S., 'The household property complex in African social organization', *Africa*, Vol. 64, No. 3, 1994.

Oesch, C., 'Coping with the effects of drought: peasant strategies and government policy. The case of Zimbabwe's communal areas', diploma dissertation, Graduate Institute of Developmental Studies, Geneva, 1993.

Okeyo, A. P., 'Daughters of the lake and rivers: Colonization and land rights of Luo women', in M. Ettiene and E. Leacock (eds), *Women and Colonization: An Anthropological Perspective*, Praeger, New York, 1980, pp. 186-213.

O'Neil, D., 'An improved stove for gari processing at the Asokwa Co-operative in Kumasi', Silsoe Research Institute, UK, 1999.

Oppong, C., *'Middle class African marriage – A family study of Ghanaian civil servants'*, Allen Unwin, London, 1981.

Redclift, M., *Sustainable Development: Exploring the Contradictions*, Routledge, London, 1987.

Reynolds, B., *The Material Culture of the Peoples of the Gwembe Valley – Kariba Studies*, Vol. 3, Manchester University Press, 1968.

Reynolds, P., *Dance Civet Cat: Child Labour in the Zambezi Valley*, Zed Books, London, 1991.

Rhoades, R., 'Participatory watershed research and management: Where the shadow falls', Gate Keepers Series No. 18, International Institute for Environment and Development, London,1998.

Salazar, M. C. and W. A. Glasinovich, (eds), 'Better Schools, Less Child Work: Child Work and Education in Brazil', Columbia, Ecuador and Guatemala, International Child Development Centre, UNICEF, Florence, 1998

Scoones, I., 'Sustainable rural livelihoods: A framework for analysis', working paper No. 72, Institute of Development Studies, University of Sussex, 1998.

Sen, A., *Poverty and Famines. An Essay on Entitlement and Deprivation*, Clarendon Press, Oxford, 1981.

Sen, A., 'Varieties of deprivation: Comments on chapters by Pujol and Hutchinson', in E. Kuiper, J. Sap et al. (eds), *Out of the Margin: Feminist Perspectives on Economics*, Routledge, London, 1995.

Silberschmidt, M., ' "Women forget that men are the masters": Gender antagonism and socio-economic change in Kisii District, Kenya', Nordic Africa Institute, Uppsala, 1999.

Spaargaren, G. and A. P. J. Mol, 'Environment, modernity and the risk society: The Apocalyptic Horizon of Environmental Reform,' *International Sociology*, Vol. 8, No. 4, 1993, pp. 217-236.

Stewart, F. G. and M. A. Amerine, *Food Science and Technology: A Series of Monographs*, Academic Press, New York, 1973.

Tambiah, S. J., 'Bridewealth and dowry revisited: The position of women in Sub-Saharan Africa and North India', *Current Anthropology*, Vol. 30, No. 4, 1989, pp. 413-436.

The Ecologist, *Whose Common Future? Reclaiming the Commons*, Earthscan Publications, London, 1993.

Thomas, E. and M. Woods, *The Manager's Casebook*, Duncan Peterson, London, 1992.

Timmer, P. C., 'Food security strategies: The Asian experience', FAO Agricultural Policy and Economic Development Series, No. 3, Rome, 1997.

UNIFEM, 'Cereal Processing', Food Cycle Technology Source Book, No. 3, United Nations Development Fund for Women, New York, 1988.

UNIFEM, 'Root Crop Processing', Food Cycle Technology Source Book, No. 5, United Nations Development Fund for Women, New York, 1989.

Van der Ploeg, J. D. and A. Long (eds), *Born From Within. Practice and Perspectives of Endogenous Rural Development*, Van Gorcum, Assen, 1994, pp. 1-7.

Van der Ploeg, J. D., *Labor, Markets and Agricultural Production*, Westview Press, Boulder, 1990.

Vickers, J., *Women and War*, Zed Books, London, 1993.

Vijfhuizen, C., 'The people you live with: Gender identities and social practices, beliefs in the livelihoods of Ndau women and men in a village with an irrigation scheme in Zimbabwe', Ph.D. thesis, Wageningen University, 1998.

Vijfhuizen, C., 'Who feeds the children? Gender ideology and the practice of plot allocation in an irrigation scheme', in E. Manzungu and P. van der Zaag (eds), *The Practice of Smallholder Irrigation: Case Studies from Zimbabwe*, University of Zimbabwe Publications, Harare, 1996.

Weinrich, A. K. H., *African Marriage in Zimbabwe*, Mambo Press, Gweru, 1982.

Wild, V., *Profit Not for Profit's Sake*, Baobab Books, Harare, 1996.

Wiskerke, H. and J. D. van der Ploeg (eds), *The dynamics of agricultural innovation at the interface of novelty creation and socio-technical regimes*, Van Gorcum, Assen, (forthcoming).

Wood, G. (ed.), *Labelling in Development Policy*, Sage, London, 1985.

Zinyama, L. M., 'Local farmer organizations and rural development in Zimbabwe', in D. R. F. Taylor and F. McKenzie (eds), *Development from Within: Survival in Rural Africa*, Routledge, London, 1992, pp. 33-44.